Solution Focused Coaching for Adolescents

Solution Focused Coaching for Adolescents explains the principles and attitude of the popular 11-step, Mission Possible, Solution Focused Coaching program for working with adolescents.

By comparing the Mission Possible principles with the 'normal' way of problem-solving in coaching scenarios, the author makes the theoretical structure and conversational style of the program easy to learn for professionals. Applied both individually and as a group activity, Mission Possible is a learning experience that makes fulfilling dreams and achieving goals easier for teenagers and young adults. It helps to make difficult things accessible for them by using one's own strengths and resources. The book is filled with detailed case studies and useful coaching tools, breaking the program down into five themes, outlining the goals, the process, and any potential pitfalls.

This practical book is intended for coaches, youth counselors, trainers, teachers, mentors, and therapists who want to coach young people using the clear step-by-step Mission Possible-program, and all those working in pastoral roles with children and adolescents.

Caroline Beumer-Peeters is an artist, published author, coach, trainer, and therapist. She is the managing director of BrandNewWay, a small impactful training institute in the Netherlands, which organizes training programs for professional educators, youth care workers, and supervisors based on a Solution Focused approach.

Solution Focused Coaching for Adolescents

Overcoming Emotional and Behavioral Problems

Caroline Beumer-Peeters

Routledge
Taylor & Francis Group

LONDON AND NEW YORK

First published 2021
by Routledge
2 Park Square, Milton Park, Abingdon, Oxon OX14 4RN

and by Routledge
605 Third Avenue, New York, NY 10158

Routledge is an imprint of the Taylor & Francis Group, an informa business

© 2021 Caroline Beumer-Peeters

British Library Cataloguing-in-Publication Data
A catalogue record for this book is available from the British Library

Library of Congress Cataloging-in-Publication Data
Names: Beumer-Peeters, Caroline, author.
Title: Solution focused coaching for adolescents : overcoming
    emotional and behavioral problems / Caroline Beumer-Peeters.
Description: 1 Edition. | New York : Routledge, 2021. | Includes
    bibliographical references and index.
Identifiers: LCCN 2020053764 (print) | LCCN 2020053765 (ebook) |
    ISBN 9780367747299 (hardback) | ISBN 9780367747237 (paperback) |
    ISBN 9781003159261 (ebook)
Subjects: LCSH: Personal coaching. | Adolescent psychology. |
    Solution-focused therapy.
Classification: LCC BF637.P36 B48 2021 (print) | LCC BF637.P36 (ebook) |
    DDC 158.3—dc23
LC record available at https://lccn.loc.gov/2020053764
LC ebook record available at https://lccn.loc.gov/2020053765

ISBN: 978-0-367-74729-9 (hbk)
ISBN: 978-0-367-74723-7 (pbk)
ISBN: 978-1-003-15926-1 (ebk)

Typeset in Sabon
by Apex CoVantage, LLC

Original idea of a 16-step Mission Possible-program: Dr. Ben Furman. New Dutch
and English version: Caroline Beumer-Peeters

Illustrations © Sieger Zuidersma

With gratitude to Ben Furman, An, Jos, Jason, Suze Beumer, and Nishant

And last but certainly not least, my thanks go to the beautiful young people who gave me their trust to travel together on this journey of discovery. You provided the insights and the material on which this program and the books are based.

Contents

Foreword

Ben Furman

Adolescents tend to have problems. At some point in their development, many of these young people will need outside support and guidance. However, helping adolescents is not easy. Adolescents seem to be almost allergic to adults telling them what to do, how to behave, or how to think. Teenagers are an embodiment of self-determination. If we try to push them by imposing our ideas on them, they will resist. If, on the other hand, we *support* them in achieving what they want to achieve, we will be more likely to be able to help them.

The key to working with adolescents is *motivation*. Do you recall the old light bulb joke? The question is: "How many psychotherapists does it take to change a light bulb?" The answer is, "Just one, but the light bulb has to want to change!"

You can achieve a lot with adolescents, but the way you work with them needs to be based on their intrinsic motivation to change something about themselves or their life. The Mission Possible-program is based on a simple theory of motivation that consists of just a few core truths.

The first truth: in order for us human beings to want to change, we need to feel that the change is what *we* want, that it is something that we consider to be of value to us.

The second truth: we need to believe that we can do it. We need to have reasons to feel confident that it is possible for us to achieve our goal and that we are able to accomplish the desired change.

The third truth: we need to feel that we are making progress, that we are not standing still but moving steadily and swiftly in the right direction.

Mission Possible is founded on these three basic truths. In this model, you do not impose your ideas on adolescents. Instead, you ask them about their dreams and hopes; you respect whatever it is that they dream of in their lives (as long, of course, as it is nothing immoral or unethical). Then you ask them to think about what it is that they would like to change in order to make their dreams come true. Adolescents get to decide their own goals. The initial motivation is ensured by the fact that their goal is associated with their own dreams about their own future, *not* expectations dictated by someone else.

As soon as the goal is set, we can take advantage of the second basic truth: to have the necessary motivation to achieve our goals, we need to trust that we can do it. Each of the following steps of Mission Possible helps build the adolescent's confidence in achieving the goal. The adolescent explores previous success, discovers hidden resources, becomes aware of progress he's already made. He recruits supporters, creates an action plan based on small, achievable steps … The goal starts looking realistic. It begins to look like something that is both worth achieving as well as doable.

For young people, their friends are highly influential – for good as well as for bad. Friends can take them down and friends can lift them up. In Mission Possible, friends are regarded as a resource. All key friends are invited to participate in supporting the adolescents. When the friends of the adolescent are focused on acting as supporters, they contribute to success. Also, with these key friends as supporters, there's a minimum risk that they'll inadvertently counteract positive developments.

Once the project is launched and in progress, you will want to make sure it will continue until the goal is achieved. The third basic truth reminds us that we need to help adolescents feel that they are making progress. Motivation may fade *unless* it is nurtured by experiences of success. In Mission Possible, it is your task to help the adolescent pay attention and notice progress. He needs to see major achievements as well as all those less remarkable small steps that are evidence of gradual progress. Success will be highlighted, and information about positive development will be regularly shared within the community of supporters.

We are certain that, if applied consistently, Mission Possible will become a useful tool for your work with young people. It is a simple step-by-step procedure, not a secret technique or strategy to be used on adolescents. It's a user-friendly and transparent model that you can share openly with the young persons you work with. And although the step-by-step structure is clear, we trust that you will find that there is still a lot of room for your creativity, personalization, and fun.

About Ben Furman

Ben Furman is a Finnish psychiatrist, psychotherapist, and author of several books that have been translated all over the world. He's an associate director of the Helsinki Brief Therapy Institute and for years hosted his own talk show on Finnish television, talking about a variety of topics on psychology. He is the inventor of the Kids'Skills method, an innovative program for problem solving for children. He is a renowned international keynote speaker as a teacher and expert on Solution Focused therapy, problem solving, children's issues, team development, systemic thinking, and personal growth.

Prologue

In the millennium year 2000, when by chance *Kids'Skills: The solution-oriented approach to solving children's problems* (by Ben Furman) crossed my path at a particularly challenging time in my life, I knew immediately I had stumbled upon something remarkable. It soon became clear to me that I was ready to embrace this different way of thinking. Kids'Skills, and Solution Focused thinking in general, was for me a new way of thinking and living, with surprising results every time. Sometimes baffling, sometimes touching, and always unique – as unique as every child and adult with whom I am fortunate to work.

No outcome is predictable, no path to any solution ever the same. I had to learn to get used to that. Result oriented and always thinking of solutions instead of problems, I was used to focus most of the time directly on the goal. Only ... whose goal, whose solution?

Fortunately, it only took a short while before I felt at ease with 'working from not-knowing'. I also felt greatly supported by my own creative background as well as the wise lessons of good friend and mentor Nishant Matthews (author of *The Friend*) and the legacy of Osho, an enlightened Indian master.

My initial doubt revealed itself as my own fear of losing control, of being powerless during the process, of 'doing it wrong'. Once I let go of all of that, a refreshing relaxation quickly set in, and I experienced a new spaciousness. It was not about me – the coach/therapist – taking on the problem and providing the solution.

With the Mission Possible-program, my only task is to focus fully on the client so that the client's process can unfold. How? Just by being present, by being unconditionally available, with genuine interest in the client. And by opening up to anything that unfolds in that particular moment – in the other, in me, and in the interaction between us – with the absolute trust that *I* don't need to know. I just need to trust that at some point, all the information and answers required will emerge from the universal field of infinite creativity that we all are part of.

It turned out to be so much nicer to work with those – young and old – who take responsibility for their problems and are willing to explore and discover their own solutions. To work with children, teenagers, and adults who wholeheartedly and with growing confidence let themselves become inspired to take new steps on their path of development and work toward a preferred goal. Every meeting and each person are unique; every session with the intention to fully meet their personal need; often with regained confidence and moments of great pleasure. The relaxation is enormous when, in the moment, I let go of my need to analyze the cause of a client's problem. Their feelings of guilt and shame dissolve. And where talking about problems and their possible cause only creates contraction and anxiety, the question "How would you like it to be different?" creates infinite space for reflection and exploration of the client's own wishes and possibilities.

After working with Kids'Skills, I noticed my own need to make this program available to young people, too. Some time before, Ben Furman had designed a small program called Mission Possible precisely for this age group. However, he developed Mission Possible specifically for young people in residential care. And when I started to work with it in an independent practice, it proved less suitable for working outside such a care structure. With Ben's approval, I started to intensively research the possibilities on a trial-and-error basis in order to find a more workable, broad-spectrum adaptation of the program. The result lies here before you.

With Kids'Skills, it's almost always possible to count on the willing participation of young children. But the Mission Possible-program unconditionally focuses on the equality of the relationship with the client and cooperation between the client and the coach. This is a much more mature approach, in which the process relies on building a solid platform for autonomous motivation. This step became step 0.

This book is written for all coaches, therapists, teachers, and counsellors who are interested in working Solution Focused with the Mission Possible-program. It is for those who want to discover how it can be used in different situations and with different types of clients. It aims to provide both insights into the 11 steps of the program as well as help you manage and guide developmental processes in young people. In fact, this book is intended for anyone who wants to invite and mobilize latent motivation for change. It's precisely this latent motivation that helps young people to empower the personal development that is so essential to their growth.

This book is designed as a practical guide to accompany the Mission Possible workbook. It's a book that, like Ben Furman's book *on Kids'Skills*, is a useful collection of steps as guidelines, background information, ideas, stories, case studies, and suggestions to make your work with this attractive age group both enjoyable and as fruitful as possible.

Since I realize very well that this book is by no means complete and may leave you with many questions unanswered, I've included a list of additional books. These I wholeheartedly recommend, because I've found them to be useful while working with this program.

About the latest revision

In 2017, I was asked to have the Mission Possible-program and textbook translated into English. This brought me to realize that after working extensively with the program for almost a decade, an update was needed. On trial-and-error basis, the program has become more refined according to the latest scientific research on motivation, new insights, and practical solutions found during my years of working with clients and students.

Now maybe more than ever, as Bob Dylan already sang in the late sixties, the times are changing. The world of young people changes as rapidly as the technological developments of our society. The Mission Possible-program needs to be able to meet those changes and stay tuned. The revised program fits their reality as much as possible. Also, some new and very useful tools have been added to make the work with Mission Possible easier for coaches. I truly hope, with this new version, to give you a helpful addition to your work with young people.

In this book, I have made a number of choices about how to address the reader. I've chosen to write on a relaxed first-name basis. The 'Solution Focused world' is an informal one. And so it should be, since the aim is to work from a position of equality as much as possible. I also chose to write this book from the perspective of the coach. Whatever the background of the user of this book and the Mission Possible workbook, a coaching attitude best encourages cooperation. As a teacher, support teacher, or therapist, you work together with your pupil or client within this approach, even if the client is not yet adult. That's why I use the word 'coach' in a broader sense, referring less to the function than to the required attitude. Therefore, I use the word 'client' where the person receiving coaching is concerned, without differentiating between children, young people, or adults. For convenience and readability of the text, I refer to this client as 'he'. I'm sure you will always be able to relate this to both sexes.

Preface

Mission Possible, a personal development program for young people

This powerful yet simple program consists of 11 steps or tasks that can help young people to set goals and achieve them successfully. Working with Mission Possible is a learning experience that makes it much easier to fulfill dreams and achieve goals. The steps guide the process of learning how to change difficult things by using the client's strengths and working with one's own resources. Like Kids'Skills, it's a program based on the Solution Focused approach. This is a way of thinking that is discussed in more detail in the next chapter. The program is designed for use under the guidance of a Mission Possible coach or therapist and is developed specifically for young people in the age group of approximately 11 to 23.

Applicable in all settings

The Mission Possible-program can be used with individual clients as well as in a group setting. When used in a group, it is possible to choose a mutual goal, or each participant can work on his individual goals. In this latter case, the group members help each other and are each other's supporters. How this is done will gradually become clearer as you read through this book.

When you don't have a key, every door feels like a wall. But as soon as you discover the keys and gain understanding, a door becomes a gateway that, even with a gentle touch, invites you and allows you in.

—Nishant Matthews

Chapter 1

Introduction

The Solution Focused approach

Not so long ago, psychology and education worked from a model that was focused on weaknesses, shortcomings, and imperfections in human behavior. The prime focus was on investigating possible causes and 'repairing' the damage caused by trauma and congenital abnormalities. In education, the focus was mainly on conditioning and unlearning undesirable behavior. These goals were achieved primarily through correction and punishment.

There was little research on healthy human functioning. Solutions were usually found by trying to understand the negative behavior. As a result, relatively very little was known about the desired healthy behavior.

Fortunately, recent years have seen distinct positive developments in such ways of thinking and working. Thanks to some remarkable pioneers, better alternatives are now available. Originally based on the Solution Focused psychology of Milton Erickson, appreciative inquiry and positive psychology, Mission Possible is such an alternative.

Basics of the Solution Focused model

Actually, the basic principles of the Solution Focused model are relatively simple. Instead of paying attention to the problem the client presents, the Solution Focused coach asks questions about exceptions (to the problem) and looks for any signs of improvement that may already have taken place.

New paradigm

After all, it's not as if the problem is evident all the time. It is the coach's job to help define the preferred changes or goals that will alleviate the problem. The coach helps the client to identify any sign of improvement that is already happening. An effective way to achieve this is to help the client describe what happens exactly at those times when the problem does not occur. The only rule without any exception is the rule that there's always an exception to a problem!

This approach, involving a detailed analysis of what is already going well and what causes it to go well, provides much useful information. This is contrary to the method preferred by many people. Indeed, it is still a global habit to first analyze what is wrong. That's great when one is suffering from illness or being faced with a technical problem but less effective or even counterproductive when dealing with problems of a more social or psychological nature.

Resource based

The coach helps the client to discover his inner resources and therefore reveal any information that supports him in reaching his goals. Resources are all the abilities and qualities a person has, as well as his previous experiences (good or bad). It doesn't matter whether these experiences have been successful. They have all, in some way, been educational and have added to the client's ability to find solutions. The Solution Focused model assumes that clients – whether they are children or adults – already possess all the resources needed to solve their problems. The only thing 'missing' is the necessary awareness or insight to apply these resources in that particular situation. The Solution Focused coach helps the client to become aware of these resources and invites him to put this newly acquired awareness into practice. This is how the coach guides the client to bring about the desired changes himself.

Doing what works

There's no 'right' way of looking at things. Different principles and methods can work equally well. The client chooses where to start, and the coach follows. A detailed analysis of the problem and its cause is seldom helpful in finding solutions. Besides, this approach often creates a number of undesirable features such as a negative frame of mind, accusatory statements, and defensive explanations.

The vicious problem circle

In describing the problem and analyzing the underlying causes, automatically, someone or something is found 'guilty'. If the cause is a person, then emotions immediately start playing their part: the accused feels the need to defend himself. Anyone who has ever found himself at any time in such a situation – and who hasn't? – knows how challenging it then becomes to work on solutions in a positive state of mind. To a large extent, emotions then determine the further course of the process toward a solution. Emotions limit the creative search for useful solutions, and even then, the search requires a lot of time and energy. Usually in such cases, the best result that may be expected is a compromise, something in the middle that's acceptable to all involved. After all, everybody should be respected and appeased! Since a compromise is rarely a completely satisfying solution for all parties, there's a good chance the compromise will result in parts of the problem remaining and new problems arising in the future.

This creates a vicious problem circle:

1   Describing problems
2   Explaining problems and finding causes
3   Using accusatory explanations
4   Defensiveness and counteraccusations (or rejecting responsibility)
5   Creating a bad mood; no willingness to collaborate
6   No creative solutions or just compromises
7   Emergence of lack of progress and new problems
8   Describing and explaining new problems and lack of progress, and so on ...

From problem to progress

Here is a schematic representation of the process in the problem-focused approach, the opposite of the Solution Focused model. This traditional problem-solving model still keeps people around the world trapped on a

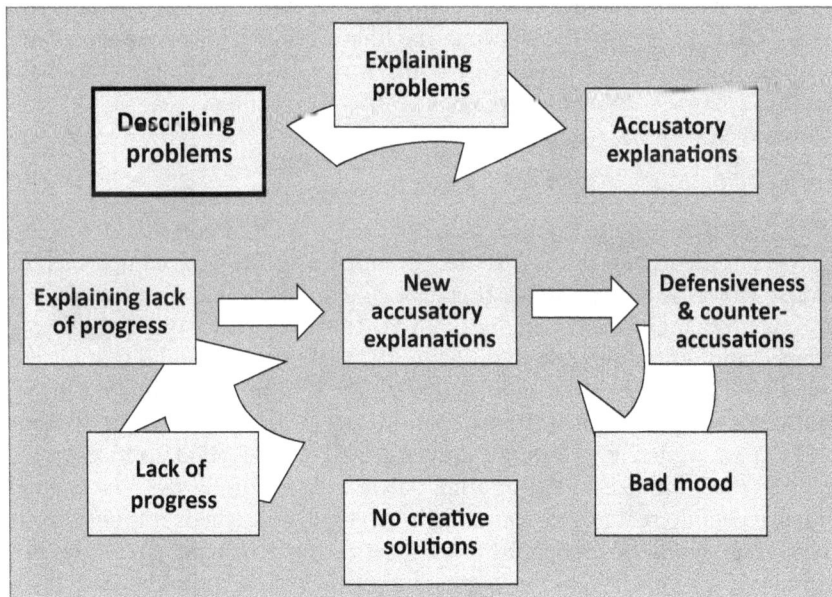

Figure 1.1 The vicious problem-circle

Source: Modified from: ©Ben Furman & Tapani Ahola, *Change through Cooperation: Handbook of Reteaming*

daily basis, even though Albert Einstein long ago proposed that problems are rarely solved with the same way of thinking that created them. He believed that if you do something that doesn't work, it is better to stop doing it and do something else instead. This seems in itself very obvious, and yet it is not what usually seems to happen. In 2002, Mark McKergow and Paul Jackson, two brilliant English pioneers in the Solution Focused approach within organizations, added these beautifully concise words: "*Change your doing, or change your viewing!*" (*The Solutions Focus: The simple way to positive change*, 2002). Meaning as much as "change what you do, or change the way you look, think and feel." Allowing yourself simply to look and think in a different way is often enough to see new possibilities. I once heard that Mother Teresa, who during her life took care of the poorest in the slums of Kolkata, was asked in an interview how she could sustain her heavy work. She replied that she saw God in all people, but that in the case of these poor people, God just has a dirty face that needs some loving attention!

Problems compared to solutions

It seems a good idea at the beginning of this book to put both the problem-focused and Solution Focused approach next to each other so the differences become clearly visible.

The first difference to catch your eyes might be that in a problem-focused model, you mainly tend to look at the past. Trying to analyze the problem in search of what caused it to occur, the focus is on what has happened and how things derailed. Therefore, it is hard to withstand the temptation of finding a 'cause' and blaming the one who's responsible.

Analyzing problems ≠ solutions

When children get into arguments, one of the most common things you can hear them say is, "He started it!" But even if 'he' indeed started it, which of course is a possibility, things can get really complicated from there. In the argument, blaming and shaming often leads to more than one party being blamed and refusing to take responsibility. Was it the child who first hit the other child? Or was it the child that took the other's toy in the first place, without asking? Or was it the parent who taught their child to hit another child in an argument? Or could it even have been the children looking on and cheering for one of the fighting parties. By analyzing the past events, you can get into real murky waters trying to figure out who is responsible. In most cases, it will be quite hard to even get the facts straight. Memories are fallible, and perception of the 'truth' is in the eye of the beholder. An objective analysis of the event is rarely possible. Ask three children arguing what has happened, and you get three different versions of the story.

Steering away from the past

When looking at this situation from a Solution Focused standpoint, the focus is on what is here now. In the example of the three children, it is three arguing children who seem to disagree on something. When first giving some space for and acknowledgment of all emotions, you almost directly focus on the preferred future. The most relevant question is here: 'What would the desired situation look like? From where the children are now, what would you and all involved want to see happen instead of the problem?'

Complexity versus simplicity

Instead of controlling the situation, for instance by punishing the children, you try to cooperate and influence the situation. In that way, the children are able to calm down, and because no one is being blamed, it becomes easier to speak about possible positive and useful solutions. Nobody needs to feel personally attacked and have a defensive response. In this way, you prevent ugly complications such as escalating emotions, more accusations, or someone bringing up the past. These things all complicate the problem and the process of solving the situation, as you can see in the mechanism of the 'vicious problem circle'.

To put it very simply:

• Don't fix what isn't broken.
• Find what works, and do more of it.
• Identify what no longer works and stop doing it.
• And do something else instead.

Waiting for the world to change

In the Solution Focused approach, you don't need to keep yourself occupied with all the deficits and imperfections, and with that, you can almost always bypass any diagnoses.

The latter is something to get used to, both for professionals and for parents. In the current system, professionals often find themselves in a sort of split. They work from the problem focus, which needs the diagnosis as an explanation of the problem. Or they *do* work Solution Focused, but they still need the diagnosis for official indication purposes to mobilize the required support and get the necessary budget available. Nowadays, this can still lead to awkward situations that hopefully will change in the near future. Until then, professionals working with children and adolescents will unfortunately have to live with this ambiguity.

Putting an end to blame

For the parents of children with problems, the diagnosis often has a completely different meaning. For them, it is an important milestone on the way to recognition of the problem and their need for help. The diagnosis also provides a more tangible explanation for the problem and provides a kind of proof of their innocence. Because of the official diagnosis, they are, at least in part, relieved of feeling like they are bad parents who have failed in raising their child. For most parents, it is very painful to have to admit that their child has problems and they need help in solving the situation that has arisen, which of course is very understandable. Because of the emotional importance often attached to the diagnosis by parents, it is sometimes difficult for them to make the switch to a different focus, away from the problem. When parents meet with a coach who listens attentively and gives them the opportunity to tell their story and share their feelings, so that they feel heard and understood, they will soon feel at ease with the Solution Focused approach. In this way, they can experience that it is also a relief for them to work together with their child to improve the problems. In this cooperation, the participants concentrate on what is going well instead of looking at what went wrong and what's missing.

Positive outlook

Progress on the way to reaching the desired outcome is accurately recorded and celebrated. The emphasis here is on simplicity, in which only small changes are necessary to achieve major effects. Because of this positive orientation, all parties involved feel positively encouraged and valued.

In short, it would be true to say that a focus on problems tends to concentrate mainly on:

- What happened? (the past)
- What's wrong?
- Who or what is the possible cause, and who is guilty?
- Faults and deficiencies
- Gaining control of the situation
- Working from expert status (the professional caregiver knows what's best for the client)
- Preventing and solving complications
- Definitions and diagnoses

However, the Solution Focused approach concentrates mainly on:

- What is here now?
- What's a preferred outcome in the future?

- Exceptions to the problem (what works well, and what's different when the problem doesn't occur?)
- Determining and monitoring progress
- Expanding influence instead of control
- Cooperation between the client and his environment
- Recognizing and using all resources
- Simplicity (the smallest possible change and the use of simple, clear language)
- Actions (small, workable steps, aimed at a specific, preferred goal)

Ownership

The Solution Focused approach ensures that the client takes responsibility for both the problem and the solutions he chooses to adopt. The significant increase in responsibility required encourages healthy independence based on autonomous motivation. More about this will be shared after the short overview of the steps of the Mission Possible-program. It stimulates self-confidence when clients themselves are responsible for both their successes and the process. Through the equal collaboration with small, achievable goals, the client experiences that there is a profit to be made by taking steps. It is worth the effort! For example, a static mindset turns into a growth-mindset (see Carol Dweck's book *Mindset*, 2007).

A mind set on progress

Just as the problem-focused approach leads to a static mindset of avoiding risk, rejecting responsibility, accusing, and not learning, the Solution Focused approach automatically leads to the development of a growth-mindset. Which is a mindset focused on development, inquisitive research, and a natural will to learn. The latter can be regarded as intrinsic motivation for learning, a drive based on pure interest or pleasure. The client with a growth-mindset faces challenges with much more confidence and less fear, because the underlying belief is one of being able to keep on growing. Talents, skills, and experiences, which together with the Mission Possible-program are described as resources, are only a starting point in this mindset. Growth is always possible simply by making efforts to take steps. The experience enriches the development. If you assume that it is always possible to improve yourself, you will naturally enjoy yourself when you take on new challenges. The process, the experience, is paramount.

Valuable failure

It's absolutely allowed to make mistakes. You can learn from them. From this viewpoint, making mistakes and learning from the experience gives confidence, even if the experience is one of having a setback. This seems to be true even for very young children. Every step – however small it may be – that is carried out successfully functions like a magnet for new steps that will be taken with an equally successful outcome ... and each success contributes to a growing, positive self-image and expectation pattern.

Pleasurable possibilities

Unless the problem is something like a challenging sudoku or a Rubik's cube, few people really like spending time solving problems. By definition, dealing with problems is not particularly fun, most people will tend to agree. Learning new skills or improving existing ones, working toward concrete goals – that sounds much more interesting and enjoyable and involves far less resistance. This awareness opens the door to exciting insights into the expanded world of new possibilities for growth and (self)-improvement that lies hidden behind every apparent problem.

Ancient wisdom

In the Chinese language, there are many characters that represent a whole word or a concept. The character for 'crisis' is constructed out of two separate smaller, independent characters: one means 'danger', the other 'chance' or 'opportunity'. If you look at a problem as a sort of crisis, then this ancient language seems to have long ago embodied the reality of both danger and opportunity. Which of the two it will turn out to be in the end is not always up to your choice. But if you look first from a growth-mindset at the possibilities and the opportunities that are inherent to the problem, then most problems do seem to end up in the category 'opportunity'.

What is 'working in a Solution Focused way'?

The Solution Focused model was originally developed in traditional psychotherapy but has since found its way, with considerable success, into the world of coaching and teaching. This approach has turned out to be highly accessible for and easily applied to clients in all age groups.

An alternative way

When focusing on solutions, you as a coach work with whatever is presented in the moment. You work toward the client's desired outcome with the intention of resolving his problems. The approach was initially a response to traditional psychotherapy, in which the therapist – the 'expert' – decides what the best solution is for the client. The new approach aims at cooperating with the client – who knows his situation better than anyone else – to arrive at a pragmatic and realistic solution that optimally suits the client's needs and capabilities. The result is a respectful brief therapy or coaching process that ultimately results in workable solutions. Responsibility and ownership for effecting his necessary changes remain with the client.

A little history

Working with a Solution Focused approach is, above all, pragmatic. The fundamentally simple theory has its roots in the Mental Research Institute (Palo Alto, USA), the philosophy of Wittgenstein, and even the Buddhist way of thinking. Various movements can with equal right claim to be the source of Solution Focused work, such as Dr. Milton Erickson, Steve de Shazer, and Insoo Kim Berg.

Typical Solution Focused assumptions and principles

The Solution Focused approach is based on a number of specific assumptions and basic principles. You could even call them 'prejudice'. But even then, they are, without exception, positive prejudices and assumptions.

These positive judgments form the heart of the Solution Focused approach, an approach that includes the Mission Possible-program. They form the basic attitude that is the essence of how the Solution Focused approach works. They also largely determine how the coach sees his clients. Here follows a list of the most notable principles and assumptions:

- Change is constant and inevitable ...
- Identify positive development and put the usable changes to good use by doing more of it.
- Interactions are based on cooperation.
- Resistance is not considered a useful concept.
- A detailed analysis and understanding of the problem is usually of little help in finding solutions.
- No problem occurs all the time. In finding exceptions, keys to finding solutions reveal themselves. The best way is to find what happens precisely when the problem does not occur.
- Signs of solutions are usually right in front of us. They only have to be noticed.
- There is no 'right' way of looking at things. There are many ways of looking at a situation. Different views can work just as well.
- Clients define their own goals and preferred future.
- Clients have all the necessary resources to find solutions.
- Small changes in the desired direction can be put to use with great effect. Only the smallest change is necessary. "Don't fix what isn't broken."

The most important Solution Focused tools

The Solution Focused approach has its own unique way of thinking and working. It differs radically from other methods and uses what are termed interventions. There are numerous Solution Focused tools, many of which have found their way into other currently used methods. Here is a list of the most important of these tools:

- Recognition (of problems that can be solved *and* those that cannot be solved, as well as progress toward the desired result)
- Encouragement and invitation (to talk about solutions)
- Resources (taking advantage of existing skills, experiences, and individual characteristics)
- The preferred result (the ideal future situation is discussed, negotiated, and created)
- The solution is not always directly related or proportional to the problem.
- Typical Solution Focused use of language
- Asking (instead of *telling* a client what he should do)

   Such as:

   - questions focusing on current, positive developments that precede the first coaching session
   - questions that invite the client to tell more
   - questions providing insight into the client's progress ('scaling')
   - questions eliciting more information about the goal (including special 'miracle questions', which sound like, "Imagine that you could order up a miracle …")
   - questions, concerning exceptions and alternatives
   - questions involving skills and various resources that the client possesses but is not yet aware of

- Compliments
- Support in continuing to do more of what already seems to be working well
- Negotiating and consensus agreement (about plans and next steps, for example)
- Simple language and simple, clear actions

In common with every other therapeutic method, Solution Focused work has its own broad range of tools that are used both as interventions and as a specific communication style. The specific way these tools are used in a Solution Focused approach is definitely different. There is, for example, a clear difference in the coach's response to whatever a client presents. There's a difference, too, in the timing of how these tools are used, like when it's best to talk or to be silent. And such subtle differences apply to many of the other Solution Focused techniques. Let's look now more closely at a small number of the most well-known and significant tools.

Solution and problem are not always directly proportional

There is a tendency to follow traditional beliefs and methods in analyzing problems so as to discover causes. There's a misconception that removing the cause will generally resolve the problem. Solution Focused work accepts, however, that the solution is not always so directly related to the problem. For many who are confronted with this for the first time, it can be quite a shock and even seem counterintuitive to everything they know about problems and solutions. The problem-focused approach assumes that there is a logical, coherent connection between problems and their solutions. Nevertheless, there are countless practical cases in which this logic simply does not apply and where it's necessary to apply a totally different approach. Albert Einstein was very clear when he stated that today's problems can seldom be resolved using yesterday's thinking that created the problems!

> *"Life is in essence simple, but we humans insist on complicating it."*
> *Confucius (China, 551–479 BC)*

Solution Focused language

It is abundantly clear that the language used in problem-focused coaching and therapy is radically different from that used in the Solution Focused approach. First and foremost, it's primarily focusing on the negative and occupies itself with the past; it seeks to understand the problem, with an all-too-frequent assumption that the problem will be here forever if you don't take away its cause. This creates a fixed mindset.

Solution Focused language is generally much more positive and optimistic, aimed at the future, and implying that whatever is happening now is just temporary and will pass. This is a more open-minded growth-mindset. If you consider that change is the only constant in life, then there's a good chance that a problem, too, will change. Because language is the primary tool used in therapeutic and coaching interactions, all questions are viewed as possible interventions.

Words matter

This is why language is used with great care and awareness. The attention that is being paid to the choice of language goes beyond the words;

it involves the sentence structure as well as the tone of voice and how the words are emphasized. It goes even further and includes nonverbal aspects such as facial expression, general body language, and the 'energy' that is expressed. Just as this last item – the 'energy' – is so hard to define objectively, there is a great deal about communication that is recognized as being important but is in the Western world still poorly understood let alone subject to scientific explanation. Language involves many complex layers, both conscious and subconscious, that are perceived on an equally complex range of levels. Every person hears and responds to language from a conscious yet superficial perception as well as from a subconscious inner reality that is deeply personal.

Scaling questions

Asking a client to evaluate a situation on a scale from 1 to 10 is an easy and fast way of finding out the client's perception of his current position. This sort of question is called 'scaling' and is a simple tool that all people can easily respond to. Using a visual aid – like placing the numbers 1 to 10 in a line on a paper or on the floor – can help even very young children to give information on a broad range of issues. After all, they don't need to use words to describe what's going on, but it helps them to feel more precisely. That is perhaps why scaling is one of the most significant and typical tools used in Solution Focused work. Besides helping to access useful information, scaling helps the client get a clear view of relevant issues that can then be discussed. Scaling simplifies and clarifies the task at hand and opens the door to discussion about concrete possibilities, thus helping the client to move forward.

Miracle questions

This is another remarkable and highly effective tool, ideal for clients (whether individuals or organizations) having some difficulty in describing their criteria for success. It's a form of questioning that puts the power of imagination to use. Such a question, in which the client is invited to imagine the preferred future already being here, is called a miracle question. It may sound like this: "Imagine that you could order up a miracle, and as if by magic, you've achieved your goal. What does it look like? How does it feel?"

What if … ?

Such a question can help the client on his way to defining solutions while at the same time providing an opportunity for him to commit himself to the desired result. Leaving aside the potential enormity of a problem and the associated negative feelings, the miracle question opens up the way to small, realistic, and concrete steps that together result in bringing the preferred future nearer. The question helps the client to form a picture of what the solution – the preferred future – looks like. It was Walt Disney who once said, "If you can dream it, you can make it."

Once the client has a clear picture of what he wishes to achieve, the coach can build on the miracle question with further supportive questions. Together, they translate this picture into a step-by-step series of specific, doable actions.

Questions about exceptions and alternatives

All problems include exceptions. But what precisely does this mean? Consider, for example, that happiness doesn't last forever ... Well, neither does a state of feeling unhappy last forever! It's just that there is a tendency to forget the last part while the focus is on the problems and other associated negatives. Thinking about problems tends to exclude an objective view of reality at that moment.

The exceptions in Solution Focused coaching involve directing the attention to those moments, however fleeting, when the problem is not dominating or temporarily doesn't occur at all. Those moments can be crucial sources of important information that support the steps toward resolving the issue. Besides, simply focusing awareness on the existence of such moments gives hope for improvement and confirms the value of looking more closely at these exceptions. All too often, these situations contain the keys to what the client can do to resolve his problem.

Compliments

Praise and validation in the form of compliments are significant features of a positive, growth-oriented basic attitude. The use of process-based compliments – referring to what was specifically done to make the achievement happen – plays an important role in this attitude. Recognizing and confirming how difficult the problem is for the client and positively affirming what he is already doing well encourages and motivates him to change. Simultaneously, the client feels the involvement and understanding of the coach or therapist. Compliments tend to identify and magnify what is already going satisfactorily. By asking the client to think about how key people in his life would compliment him, the coach helps him to connect with and involve the most important people outside the coach's office and, at the same time, offers a change of perspective that can bring up some interesting new views. The chapter describing Step 5 of the Mission Possible-program expands further on this topic.

Negotiation of Solution Focused goals

In Solution Focused work, everything that is done has a purpose directly related to the end result. This means that each specific step must be relevant and will be a point of discussion between coach and client. This is the reason it is so important that any goals set are clear, concrete, specific, and measurable. The solutions aimed at should be doable so that it is possible to determine when the job is done. The client clarifies with the coach when the problem is sufficiently resolved. At the same time, the client needs to have gained adequate self-confidence in order to proceed on his own after the problem has been resolved. In the absence of such specific criteria, coaching can go on for a long time before either the client or the coach becomes aware that important changes, indicating success, have actually already taken place.

Mission Possible

A brief introduction to the program

It is not so easy to find an adequate description for Mission Possible. Perhaps it is more convenient first to give a description of the method Kids'Skills, of which Mission Possible is, sort of, a 'big brother'. Then it will probably become clearer once you know the similarities and differences between the programs.

Kids'Skills, developed in Finland by Ben Furman and Tapani Ahola, is a Solution Focused method consisting of 15 simple steps, which help children to overcome even relatively large problems by inviting them to learn new skills or become better at skills they've already mastered.

Similar yet different

Mission Possible is a similar 11-step program that can help young people with finding, setting, and successfully achieving goals. Using the steps of the program, they can make the successful realization of their goals a pleasant and educational process.

In its present form, developed by Ben Furman and Caroline Beumer, Mission Possible is a Solution Focused approach for young people between the ages of approximately 11 and 23 years. Like Kids'Skills, it is based on the Solution Focused educational psychology. The program uses steps that can be used as a structure to work on problem solving, goal setting, and the successful achievement of these goals and solutions. Besides these similar possibilities to Kids'Skills, Mission Possible proves to be useful in finding goals in general and in obtaining and maintaining the motivation to work toward achieving them. For many teenagers and young adults, this usually is a challenge in daily life. In short, it's fair to say that Mission Possible is more widely applicable in all situations in which young people experience problems or in which they would like to see change happening. And it is not only useful in solving behavioral problems and fears. It is much more a personal-development program for young people, helping them to set goals and, step by step, successfully work toward them.

Taking the world by storm

Kids'Skills has proven its worth in many countries and especially enjoys great interest in the Netherlands with coaches, therapists, teachers, and counselors in primary schools. Also, Kids'Skills finds its way increasingly well into the world of child- and youthcare, healthcare, and parenting. At present, Kids'Skills is even being applied in schools in occupied Palestinian territory, where children have to deal with the traumas of an everyday reality of violence. Also, in China, interest is rising from the fields of education and social work since 2015.

> *"Find out what works, and do more of it."*

Children as co-experts

The time that solving children's problems was left only to experts seems to be over. Nowadays, every teacher is faced with children's behavioral problems in the classroom. In the current school system, these children usually go to ordinary schools. This often requires almost therapeutic skills from teachers and can be quite challenging for them, especially when classes are getting larger and many teachers experience an increase in their tasks. As a result, many teachers feel overwhelmed and overworked. I often hear that they feel burdened with responsibilities for which they are not educated and do not feel equipped. Kids'Skills and Mission Possible provide them support and bring back energy and fun while solving these problems. From across the country, I receive emails weekly from teachers who have serious concerns but, fortunately, also more and more e-mails from those who have already discovered that the Solution Focused approach works. WOWW (Insoo Kim Berg and Lee Shilts, 2002, *Working on What Works: Coaching teachers to do more of what's working*), as well as Kids'Skills and Mission Possible in particular seem to have an adequate answer here.

Mission Possible: the new kid on the block

Mission Possible, at its first publishing in 2010, didn't have the long history Kids'Skills had yet. At that time, it was still relatively unknown in the educational system. Until then, it had been used mainly in residential treatment groups in Finland, for whom it originally was designed. Yet there was, thanks to the success of Kids'Skills, an increasing interest in a similar program for teenagers and adolescents.

In the last decade, Mission Possible has acquired a solid place alongside Kids'Skills and is widely used in the structure of primary education, secondary education, youth and family care, mental healthcare, youth healthcare, and generally in coaching and therapy. This success is partly driven by the changing need for care in society, with increasing emphasis on self-reliance and personal responsibility.

Many more experienced Kids'Skills users will seamlessly switch to working with young people with the Mission Possible-program, because despite the differences, the similarities are clearly visible. Based on the same principles, it requires a similar way of thinking and acting. It is, like Kids'Skills, a step-by-step program that doesn't necessarily need to be taken in the exact order given. And it can generate just as much energy and fun.

The need to build on motivation

Yet there is an important difference with Kids'Skills. While younger children usually are naturally cooperative, this tends to be less obvious when working with older children, teenagers, and adolescents, especially when they don't come voluntarily. In such cases, it is necessary to first establish a platform for cooperation and motivation for setting goals and working toward them. For that to happen, you, the coach, need to meet them where they are. Building a solid foundation for their motivation for positive change and building the necessary trust between them and the coach is the first step to attend to before anything else can be done. In many cases, this basic trust in the cooperation with a coach is absent or damaged at the start of the program, since it already often has been disappointed. Moreover, it's very natural for teenagers and adolescents at this particular point in life to want to look at things without the help and involvement of an adult. The accompanying Mission Possible script provides tools for this need for self-direction.

A summary of the 11 steps

1 The goal

> "What do you want to learn or get better at? What would you like to achieve?"

The Mission Possible-program begins with envisioning the future. The coach asks the client to imagine for himself a preferred future, a future that seems ideal to him and in which he feels comfortable with everything – his private life, his work, or his study. This dream of the preferred future, in which his problems are resolved, is the foundation for the rest of the work with this program. Next steps include looking closely at what must happen in order to make this dream come true and the intermediate goals that will help create this future. 'Goals' here imply the concrete things that must change, specific skills that need to be learned or improved on, or tangible steps that must be undertaken. Once the coach has helped the client get clear about all these minor goals and steps, the client then decides which initial goal is the most attractive and effective. For this particular step, a protocol has been created to make it as easy as possible. In the chapter on step 1, this will be explained in detail as a 'how to'.

Step 1: The Goal
What would you like to learn, or become better at?

Step 2: The Benefits
How will it benefit you, and how will it benefit others?

Step 3: Support
Who can help you to achieve your goal?

Step 4: Symbol
What could serve as a symbol for your goal and help you to remember it?

Step 5: Trust and Confidence
What makes you and your supporters trust that you will achieve your goal?

Step 6: Resources and Optimism
What resources do you have that you can apply to achieve your goal?

Step 7: Scaling
Where, on a scale from 1 to 10, are you, on the way to achieve your goal?

Step 8: Action
What are you going to do in order to come closer to reaching your goal?

Step 9: Keeping Log
How are you going to keep track of your progress and record this?

Step 10: Preparing for Setbacks
If you encounter setbacks on the way, how are you going to tackle these?

Step 11: Celebrating success
How will you celebrate achieving your goal, and thank your supporters?

An overview of the 11 Mission Possible steps

Figure 1.2 An overview of the 11 Mission Possible steps

Source: © Caroline Beumer-Peeters

2 Benefits

> "What benefits will achieving your goal have for you, and what benefits will it have for other people?"

It is much easier for the client to choose a goal when it is clear to him what the benefits are of achieving that goal. The longer the list of benefits, the more desirable the goal becomes. After encouraging the client to imagine every possible positive consequence of achieving his goal, both for himself and for other people in his life, the idea of committing to that goal becomes increasingly more attractive and valuable.

3 Support

> "Which friends and/or members of your family could help you achieve your goal?"

The help, support, and encouragement of others are truly needed in order to achieve a goal. By asking a number of people (for example, friends and relatives) to be supportive in achieving a goal, the client creates a favorable climate for success. The client informs his supporters about his mission: setting and achieving a goal with the Mission Possible-program. He also invites them to make their own personal contribution to encourage him and, by doing so, improve his chance of success.

4 Symbol

> "What item, idol, photo, word, expression, or piece of music could symbolize your goal and help maintain your focus?"

It's very normal to have various items that have some special value or significance. It's equally human to attach a symbolic value to things as a visual representation of emotional, psychological, or spiritual values. It's a form of communication. When the client chooses for himself a symbol that represents his chosen goal, it makes that goal more tangible. A goal that seemed abstract or far away and in the future is brought closer, into the here and now, becoming a source of support and motivation. It helps that young people nowadays are increasingly familiar with visual representations that have become a significant part of their reality.

5 Trust and confidence

> "What would your supporters (friends and/or family) say that makes them confident that you can reach your goal?"

Even the defined goal not appearing to be so easy to reach does not mean that it's impossible. This step is designed to clarify the basis of trust: what is it about the client that makes him believe he can reach his goal, and what is it that helps supporters and other involved people believe he can be successful?

6 Resources: grounds for optimism

"What skills or possibilities do you (already) have that you can make use of in reaching your goal?"

Whatever the goal is that is defined, it's rarely something radically new. It often involves something that has been worked on before, in different circumstances, and, above all, with a different level of awareness. It's important to look at this previous success – or parts of it – with awareness and to both recognize and identify the skills and personality traits the client applied at that time. In this way, it becomes possible to apply the same resources in the current project – consciously. There's an additional benefit: recognizing that the right resources are already available nourishes the client's confidence that he truly can reach his goal. At the same time, a definite sense of optimism serves to remove, or at least minimize, any doubts about a successful conclusion to the project.

7 Scaling

"On a scale from 1 to 10, where would you place yourself? Where 1 indicates that you've just found out your goal, but you've not yet done anything to move toward your goal, and 10 indicates that you've already reached your goal."

This step effectively incorporates all the previous steps in a single exercise. Answering this question helps the client to become aware of every level and nuance of his project. This step is usually the one that helps him internalize his motivation. Scaling also empowers by making clear the short-term actions that bring the goal within reach.

8 Action

"What are you going to do this week to get you closer to your goal?"

While scaling, the coach helps the client look closely at possible ways of approaching the goal, of bringing it closer. Step 8 builds on step 7, making this process as concrete and specific as possible. Here the client makes a choice and, with the coach's support, commits to clear agreements about what actions he will take in the next, defined period of time.

9 Keeping log

> "How do you intend to keep track of your progress and make it visible? With whom are you going to share your logbook or blog?"

Accurate tracking of progress made toward the goal is a key part of the Mission Possible-program. It involves the client maintaining a detailed record of his progress toward reaching his goal. A written or drawn log or a digital version (privacy is then subject to discussion) helps the client to stay motivated throughout the process. It means, too, that he must be alert for all signs of progress and success, however minor. Naturally, he should be encouraged to think in a Solution Focused way by concentrating mainly on positive developments.

10 Preparing for setbacks

> "What will you do to overcome setbacks, considering setbacks are a natural part of every learning process?"

It's more or less certain that at some point in the program, the client is going to experience a setback despite all the careful attention to positive developments. Sometimes things just go differently from how they were planned or intended. Because of this reality, it's essential to plan for and 'expect the unexpected'. Anticipating such setbacks and making agreements about how to deal with them if and when they should happen is the best way to avoid disappointment and loss of motivation.

11 Celebrating success!

> "How are you going to celebrate reaching your goal? How will you show your supporters how pleased you are with their support? How will you thank them for their contribution?"

At a certain moment, it will be clear that the goal has been reached or at least that sufficient progress has been made to consider the reality of success. It's then time for the client to be proud of his achievement! Time, too, to look back at the process, consider, and be aware of how he has managed to reach this point. It's an important stage in the program when the client can take responsibility for his efforts and – where appropriate – newly acquired skills. It can also be quite revealing to realize the extent to which supporters and other people have contributed to his success. And it's the right moment to celebrate this success together with all those who have helped him and to thank them for their contribution in reaching his goal. A growing awareness of the value of gratitude can be a valuable additional feature of this part of the program.

After this brief overview of the steps of the Mission Possible-program, the next chapters will venture a little deeper into the details of each step. But before going through the 11 steps one by one, it's best to first discuss the topic of motivation and the influence on the quality of motivation of the five different themes in the Mission Possible-program.

Autonomous motivation?

In the world of care and education, much is currently being said about motivation. Everyone knows immediately what is meant by 'motivation', and all unanimously acknowledge its importance. But as soon as one tries to describe exactly what it is, it becomes a lot harder and more confusing.

Because Mission Possible, just like Kids'Skills, is fully based on generating, activating, and retaining motivation as much and effectively as possible, it seems useful to highlight this interesting topic a bit further here. A lot of research has been done about motivation, and much is being written about it. Yet there is still a lot of confusion. It's essential to know exactly what is happening in the field of motivation development in order to achieve a successful and lasting effect with coaching. If we do not understand motivation, coaches might sometimes end up doing the wrong things with the best intentions.

Building blocks of motivation

Analysis of the concept of motivation shows that three different kinds of motivation can be distinguished: intrinsic, extrinsic, and autonomous motivation. But what do these different forms exactly mean, and why is it important to be aware of this distinction? To gain better understanding on the topic of motivation, I have to start from the self-determination theory (*Intrinsic motivation and self-determination in human behavior*, 1985) by Jeff Deci and Richard Ryan, professors in psychology and social sciences (E.L. Deci & R.M. Ryan, 2016, *Self-determination theory: Basic psychological needs in motivation, development, and wellness*). This theory assumes that every person is naturally focused on growth and self-development. They also stated that three basic needs must be met for this to develop: autonomy, relationship, and competence. According to Deci and Ryan, these three basic needs are the same for all people, regardless of age and the country or culture in which they grow up. Every person learns every day. Our brains simply can't act any different, and this development continues throughout our entire lives.

Constant learning

Deci and Ryan took a proactive approach to learning with their statement about the motivation for growth and development. They argue that even in the absence of a clear goal or necessity, people are inclined to learn, purely because it gives them pleasure or interests. This latter drive for motivation is called intrinsic motivation. It refers to activities that humans do without any other purpose than our natural satisfaction and the pleasure that the activity brings us. Examples of such activities include: playing, improvising, making music, playing games, practicing a hobby or sport, and so on. The conscious reason and drive for the activity is the pleasant experience, the fun, or the curious interest. That doesn't mean that it cannot deliver anything valuable. After all, humans learn from every activity.

Driven by pleasure and interest

The typical characteristic of intrinsic motivation is that the motivation to do the activity is spontaneous, curious, and interested. It gives pleasure and energy. Babies do this already, investigating and playful from day one. And older children, even if they live in poor conditions, continue to explore curiously. Even in the animal world, this behavior is observed. Just think about the behavior of puppies and kittens. Their play is aimed at enjoying the activities, but in the meantime, they unknowingly learn skills for later. There is no reward of the activity other than pleasure at the moment. And from this last observation, it doesn't take much thinking to conclude that intrinsic motivation can also be undermined as soon as one starts tinkering with the three basic needs.

Undermining intrinsic motivation

The degree of intrinsic motivation appears to depend on the degree to which the need for autonomy, competence, and relationship is met. These three need to be somehow equally balanced. Disturbing this balance, for example by giving rewards or compliments, intrinsic motivation can be reduced. As soon as teenagers and adolescents feel that they no longer perform an activity solely because it is so much fun or interesting but because they are rewarded for it, their intrinsic motivation decreases. Many parents should realize this when they frequently compliment their children or when they promise their teenagers to pay for their driver's license training if they abstain from alcohol, drugs, or sex until adulthood. Such a promise of a reward often works counterproductively. Extrinsic motivation makes people do things because they aim for a specific goal. It leads to a precalculated and desired yield. Extrinsic motivation is therefore not necessarily more negative, worse or less valuable than intrinsic motivation, although this is often perceived this way.

Finally, what started as extrinsically motivated behavior can be internalized or may even change into intrinsically motivated behavior. If a person reads a difficult book with the purpose of learning something from the content, then his primary reason for doing this is extrinsic (because it focuses on a predetermined outcome). But while reading, it can happen that he gets totally absorbed in the content of the book and that he loses sight of the predetermined goal altogether. If we immerse ourselves so intensively in the reading material and read the book in one breath without any thought of the initially intended importance of learning, our motivation has changed and thus become intrinsic. Intrinsic motivation and extrinsic motivation are therefore two strictly separate concepts. But in daily practice, they overlap, influence, and reinforce each other.

Nature or nurture

Deci and Ryan stated in their self-determination theory that humans are strongly focused on the most important people in their environment ('significant others') and that from an early age, they try to internalize the values of their environment by internalizing them. From that moment on, the motivation to do things that conform to these values has also become important to them. They then no longer do things for the proceeds but also because they have found them to be important too. This internalized extrinsic motivation is a high form of motivation and leads to high-quality work and behavior with integrity that is consistent with the common values.

"No two people in the world are alike. They are as unique as a fingerprint. No two people understand a sentence in the same way. If you work with people, let them find their own concept of how they should be, instead of offering yours."

Autonomy

Intrinsic motivation and internalized extrinsic motivation together make motivation complete and 'autonomous'. This is the most optimal form of motivation. If a person has reached autonomous motivation for an activity, it means that he is completely behind his goal. He considers the activity and the revenue to be important to him and also enjoys it or is interested in it. Research in the context of self-determination has shown that intrinsic motivation is present throughout a person's entire life. Various positive effects are attributed to it, such as a higher degree of learning ability, productivity, creativity, and well-being. However, intrinsic motivation depends on the perception of autonomy and competence. If these two basic needs are not met, intrinsic motivation decreases.

Designed to generate and maximize motivation

In the Mission Possible-program, the steps are focused as much as possible on generating and retaining autonomous motivation (intrinsic plus internalized extrinsic motivation). Due to the equivalent character of the cooperation between the client and the coach, the first basic need for autonomy is met. The chosen goal is secured in the ownership of the client in steps 0 and 1. It is his self-chosen goal. By cooperating with the coach and the active contribution of the clients' supporters during the Mission Possible-program, his basic need for connection and relationships is fulfilled. And finally, all steps of the program are aimed at increasing self-confidence and a sense of competence. This guarantees the most important preconditions for optimal autonomous motivation during the project. For example, a young client chooses a goal for which he is both intrinsically and internalized extrinsically and therefore autonomously motivated. And if this process of becoming autonomously motivated were not fully completed at the start of the process, then all subsequent steps are aimed at acquiring this autonomous level of motivation.

Examples of different motivation

Intrinsically motivated goals are, for example forming friendships, forming intimate relationships, personal development, playing and having fun, and finding pleasure in practicing a hobby or sport. Examples of extrinsic goals include taking on an education or obtaining a diploma, applying for jobs, raising money or acquiring fame, and gaining status or power. Examples of autonomously motivated goals are making a useful or artistic contribution to the community of which we are part, such as voluntary work, seeking meaning, and all the above intrinsic and extrinsic goals that are combined.

What's the main drive?

Intrinsically motivated goals are focused on revenue that we naturally appreciate. Extrinsically motivated goals are focused on instrumental revenues. Achieving intrinsic goals immediately leads to satisfaction of the basic needs for autonomy, relationship and competence. Achieving extrinsic goals does not. This is probably the main reason the achievement of intrinsic goals in general is accompanied by a higher degree of well-being than the achievement of extrinsic goals (K.M. Sheldon & L.S. Krieger, 2014, *Walking the talk: Value importance, value enactment, and well-being*). Things such as personal growth and good relationships generally lead to a higher sense of well-being and functioning than achieving fame, wealth, and power, for example. It therefore seems only logical that working on a goal that carries all these things is most likely to be successful. Because of the inherent pleasure of working on such an autonomously motivated goal, old patterns and limiting beliefs about learning and working are also transformed. This makes it easier for young clients to start new goals and change the negative expectations of the fixed mindset of limiting beliefs into a growth-mindset.

The five themes of the Mission Possible-program

Before dealing with the 11 steps in more detail – one step per chapter – it's first necessary to understand the different themes that make up the Mission Possible-program. These themes represent and focus on the five most important psychological factors that determine achieving and sustaining optimal motivation. Together with the three basic needs from Deci and Ryan's self-determination theory, they constitute the conditions that ensure the success of the Mission Possible-program. By listing them, followed by the associated Mission Possible steps, it becomes immediately clear that the Mission Possible-program does in no way work chronological. True, they're written down in a numbered order both in this book and in the workbook. But in practice different steps are relevant simply at the right moment for the client and his process. Some steps may need to be repeated, and some can perhaps even be omitted. The methodology is subordinate to the process of the client. Remember, too, that the program is subject to the client's process – it's a flexible tool that follows and supports the client in his development and growth. Mission Possible is, above all, a program that is always tailored to the needs of the individual client: leading from one step behind the clients' shoulder.

The five themes:

1   Ownership: your goal is clear and truly yours (appropriate and desirable). Featuring steps 0, 1, and 7.
2   Value: your goal must have value for you (providing benefits). Featuring steps 2, 7, and 11.
3   Trust and confidence: you have confidence that you can reach your goal (achievable). Featuring steps 3, 4, 5, 6, 7, and 11.
4   Observing and monitoring success: you can experience positive development (progress focused). Featuring steps 7, 8, 9, and 11.
5   Anticipating setbacks: you are well prepared for any setbacks (failing is learning, a growth-mindset). Featuring step 10.

Ownership

The first theme is about ownership by the client and choosing a preferred goal. The Mission Possible steps 0, 1, and 7 are aiming entirely at investigating what is important for the young client himself. What problems he experiences and what solutions he sees as useful for this are the subject of discussion here. Which parts of the goal are already fully or partially present and which experiences from the past could be useful now is here being examined in detail. Together with the coach, the client examines how he relates to the preferred goal and how he himself bears responsibility for the outcomes. The clearer and more concrete the goal in this step is described, the better. This prevents the setting of unrealistic or too-vague objectives and keeps the risk of failure as small as possible.

Of course, you want young clients in all cases to actually achieve their goal with success. Or that they can at least get to a point where they can proudly look back on what they have achieved in their Mission Possible-program so that they can see a major improvement of their problem and positive developments toward a preferred future. A new disappointing experience naturally detracts from their motivation.

And that is not just for young clients. Every person wants to see something come out of his efforts. If the goal is completely clear and concrete in this phase, it will come to life, and it will be easier for them to see what is needed to achieve it. The specific description of the goal marks the end of this process. It is the prelude to the second theme, in which the value of the goal is examined.

The value of the goal

The second theme includes the Mission Possible steps 2, 7, and 11. These steps are aimed at recognizing and clarifying the value of successfully achieving the goal. Two sorts of benefits can be distinguished: benefits for your client and benefits for his environment. The more benefits there are, the greater the extrinsic motivation. Benefits that touch upon the internalized values of the environment make the motivation internalized extrinsic. This further identification with the goal and the expected positive consequences that the achievement of the goal will have for him helps the client to be motivated to start the program. The question "But what do I get out of it?" is a genuine question. Why should he do something if he is not convinced in advance that it will really bring him something worth the while? Whether that worth is a concrete outcome or only the pleasure of the experience doesn't matter.

In these first two themes, therefore, two important factors for motivation become clear:

1   Ownership: "*It is my goal.*"

    We can link this psychological factor to the need for autonomy.
    "*I can choose what is important to me, what things I will learn, and how I want to shape my future.*"

2   Value: "*The goal has benefits for me.*"

    This is a psychological factor that relates to all three basic needs from the self-determination theory: autonomy, relationship, and competence.
    "*I decide and do it myself. It provides benefits for me as well as for my environment. I learn new skills or improve existing ones, solve my problems, and work on my own future.*"

A case study from practice: Josh and Marsha

On a weekday, Josh (16) and Marsha (15), whom you will be meeting on more than one occasion in this book, come to the practice accompanied by their mother, Inez. She has asked for counseling with me because the home situation between Josh and Marsha has become quite untenable. The (according to their mother) insecure Marsha is constantly picked on by her rather domineering older brother. This provides a lot of hassle and frustration, and this regularly leads to a scuffle between the two.

Listening to all sides

Upon entering the practice room, they both give me a decent handshake and are giggling with each other some. Despite their problems, they seem to be a happy and committed sibling couple. There is a clear difference in presentation between brother and sister. Marsha looks a bit shy, smiles down at the floor, and mumbles her name softly and almost unintelligibly. Josh, with happy and a bit cheeky eyes from under his baseball cap, smiles at me and takes in the situation. He allows himself almost immediately to fall into the most comfortable-looking chair so that his mother and sister have to settle for whatever seats are left. With wide-spread legs and seemingly relaxed, he sits leaning back and watches while his mother and sister, still somewhat unaccustomed, are sitting down too.

Rising irritation

Their mother says that at home, many arguments are being made and that these more and more often include an exchange of punches. Because Josh and Marsha are already so big, their mother fears she is not able to control the situation much longer. Inquiry with the two adolescents delivers the following version of the story. Josh says he is particularly annoyed at his sister because she is so insecure. He is annoyed at everything she does. He frankly admits that he actually gets annoyed by 'everything anyway'. It doesn't really matter too much what others do. He's always quickly irritated. Then he gets angry and starts teasing her. His unacceptable behavior can be anything; from farting in her face as they walk up the stairs, pushing and letting her trip intentionally, taking away Marsha's belongings, stealing and hiding or destroying them, and even pawing her at times. Lately it happens more often that Marsha then runs away screaming and crying or they begin to beat and kick each other. Marsha confirms the story, a little giggly, and keeps to her silence. Also, her mother nods with ashamed red cheeks that this is indeed usually how it goes. Josh doesn't seem to care very much that he doesn't play such a fair role in the story. The annoying behavior of others is, in his eyes, much worse than his own.

Talking about the preferred future

After this introduction, the four of us discuss together, instead of the current situation, what they would like to see happen instead. Mother and Marsha agree with each other and are able to describe their desired situation. Clearly, they both want Josh to pay less attention to the behavior of other family members, in particular that of Marsha, and to stay away from her. They also want Josh not to increasingly interfere everywhere. Then there is no irritation and no need to fight anymore. However, Josh finds all this to be great nonsense. He just wants the others not to do things he resents. But because Mother and Marsha say Josh feels bothered by everything and everyone, even very normal behavior, this quickly becomes a deal breaker in the negotiations.

Benefits

Josh keeps up his responsibility-rejecting attitude until I ask him what advantages it would have for him if the situation would be different, more like the desired situation of Mother and Marsha. After initially becoming a little fidgety, he seems willing to think about it. And soon he is able to mention some benefits. First, he mentions getting less punishment as a great advantage. But then he really is off for a good start and calls the lack of injuries such as scratches and bitemarks an additional benefit. And he is able to imagine that it will result in more peacefulness and less stress if he no longer interferes with the others and gets less quickly annoyed about them. The time saved he would like to apply on nice activities, such as time on his computer for gaming and chatting with his peers on social media. These are his activities that suffer regularly from the many punishments Mother feels inclined to force upon him. Also, he is able to imagine more peace in the house will help his mother to feel happier, and this will benefit everyone else.

The absence of disadvantages

And so gradually, Josh's list of benefits becomes longer and longer, much longer than the list of advantages of the undesired behavior brings him. Josh starts to realize there's also a long list of disadvantages to his behavior, disadvantages he actually had never consciously taken into consideration. From that moment on, he says, together with his sister and mother, a resounding 'yes' to working toward a mutual goal with the Mission Possible-program. We agree on setting a positive goal together when we meet the next time.

Trust and confidence

The third theme consists of the Mission Possible steps 3 through 7 and step 11, which are all designed to strengthen the client's belief in his inherent abilities. This is the third important psychological factor for achieving optimal motivation: having the confidence that you can do it! In order to be optimistic about his ability to achieve a goal, a client needs the confidence that he has the necessary resources. And because of past negative experiences, clients are not always unconditionally convinced of their reasons for optimism, so they need as much persuasion as possible. The coach can often help the client by making use of existing resources, such as highlighting previous success, or creating the conditions for unknown resources to emerge. By using as many resources as possible in these six steps, it becomes obvious to the client that nobody has to start from scratch. Almost always, a lot is already present and achieved that gives rise to confidence in the client's own abilities and a good outcome.

In this third theme, therefore, two important factors for motivation become clear:

3   Confidence and trust: "*I am confident that I'm able to reach my goal. I also know other people, like family and friends, trust me to be successful.*"

This is a psychological factor that relates to two of the basic needs from the self-determination theory: the need for relationship and a sense of competence. "*I'm not alone in this. Other people support me on my journey. I have confidence in myself. I've learned other skills before and reached many goals already. Therefore, I have good reason to believe I can be successful this time, too.*"

Observing and monitoring success

The prime focus of the fourth theme, which is represented in steps 7, 8, 9, and 11, involves consciously experiencing and relishing any and all progress made. To stay motivated during the whole program, it's essential for the client to witness both his progress and the success that he achieves. However minor progress and success may appear to be, it's crucial to the motivation process to pay attention to them. It's all too easy to underestimate how quickly frustration can rob a client of his motivation to persevere and move forward. The fourth vital factor for optimal motivation is, therefore, the ability simply to see that progress is being made! That's one of the reasons it's so useful to discuss celebrating success, even at a very early stage in the program, and build on the assumption that success will be forthcoming.

In this fourth theme, therefore, two important factors for motivation become clear:

4 Recognizing and monitoring progress: "*I'm moving forward and getting, step by step, nearer to my goal.*"

This is a psychological factor that relates to all three basic needs from the self-determination theory: autonomy, relationship, and competence.

"*I did it myself, and I see my progress as the effect of and as a reward for my effort. I perceive myself as successful. I'm able to feel proud of myself. I feel my supporters are proud of me, and I am grateful for their contribution.*"

Anticipating possible setbacks

And finally, the fifth theme pays primary attention to the balance between celebrating the ultimate success (reaching the planned goal) on the one hand, and, on the other hand, anticipating possible setbacks by making plans for concrete actions ready to implement. Talking about setbacks – as a realistic and mostly unavoidable part of the learning process – is a crucial part of ultimate success. If the coach forgets to broach this subject, the possibility is high that unexpected setbacks will disastrously affect motivation and perseverance. The disappointment of a sudden and unexpected setback or downturn can be especially painful in a euphoric period of progress.

Such disappointment of a new negative experience can, indeed, lead to a withdrawal from further action and completely sabotage any confidence that there was in the possibility of success and the achievement of the planned goal. The fixed mindset of "You see, I can't do it, I'll never succeed," must change into a growth-mindset: "OK, I made a mistake or had a setback, but I know now what to do in the future. I've learned from the experience." Failure equals learning. And with that mindset, adversity becomes a success experience inevitably leading to progress. Step 10 reframes mistakes and setbacks as an inseparable and valuable part of every learning process. With that understood, the client can go on to experience step 11, celebrating success, fully and confidently.

In this fifth theme, therefore, one more crucial factor for motivation becomes clear:

5 Anticipating setbacks: "*I'm prepared for moments of setback and adversity. Setbacks are a normal part of learning. And I've made a plan to get back on track.*" This is a factor that relates to all three basic needs from the self-determination theory: autonomy, relationship, and competence.

"*I know what to do to get myself back on track when times are tough. Everybody experiences setbacks. In case of adversity, I have a plan and know where to go for help. I'm prepared and able to handle the*" *situation. I can feel disappointed, and I know this is only temporary. Progress will eventually come."*

The following example may help clarify these five themes: ownership, value, confidence and trust, recognizing and monitoring progress, and anticipating setbacks.

A case study from school: high-school student

Imagine a high-school student who must write an essay for his course on society and culture. The choice of topic is up to him, but before starting writing, he must first select a suitable subject. It is, however, important to ensure that writing the essay really is a free choice and not just a way of conforming to a requirement set by the teacher. But how can this be achieved? What is the source of the student's motivation?

A valuable first step for the student is to look at what he considers important and relevant in his own life in the broader context of society and culture. Numerous questions arise, such as:

• What are his current opinions?
• How does he view the future in the light of this subject?
• What is his standpoint in relation to the society in which he lives?
• Are there any personal benefits to exploring this specific topic further?

Once he is aware of where his interests lie and what he considers important, it will be far easier to select a relevant topic to write about. In this way, the topic starts to have some personal, intrinsic value and significance for the student – it becomes more than just a homework assignment.

The student's next step is to look closely at what possibilities (tools, skills, insights, information) he already has to write an essay that is both useful and satisfying.

A basic skill is soon established – the ability to write! Maybe he also has the use of a computer and access to the Internet for further research into the subject. Consider, too, that in the past, he has already written essays that have been well received and given good grades.

Imagine also that the teacher expresses his confidence in the quality of the resulting essays based on the enthusiastic discussions that have regularly taken place in the classroom. Yes, he has high expectations because of the interest that the students have already demonstrated.

Although the whole class thinks it's a tough assignment, when they start talking about it together, they discover a willingness to help each other. The students agree to meet up regularly to exchange information and also that advice and feedback will be offered. They quickly see that everyone can benefit, can check on their progress and get valuable input; after all, two heads know more than one!

The students also agree to help each other so that if one student – for whatever reason – starts to lag behind or run into difficulties, he'll be supported. A student who is less skilled at writing will also get assistance to ensure he completes the task. They agree, too, that email is perhaps the best way to keep in touch. By email, they can share their draft essays and give feedback and suggestions as to how to proceed. The digitally smart students offer to give technical support to everyone who thinks he might need it.

In this cooperative way, together, the students ensure that the assignment is completed and delivered on time – to everyone's satisfaction!

Chapter 2

A solid platform for motivation

Step 0: Becoming a customer for change

Before starting to apply the Mission Possible-program with a new client, there's usually an important preparational step required. Let's call this Step 0, because it forms the foundation for motivation, trust, and the possibility of fruitful cooperation between the client and the coach.

Although it's not formally described as a step in the Mission Possible-program, it is perhaps the most essential. Building a solid base for motivation is the foundation for the entire project. Compare with any building that is constructed without a strong foundation – it's destined for a short life span, let alone the risk that the building will never be completed and actually lived in. The client's ownership of his problems as well as his solutions is the best starting point for successful change. A healthy basis for successful cooperation during the process exists only from the moment the client takes full responsibility for both problem and solution.

Creating optimal motivation

A key question for all coaches is: "How do I ensure that my clients – who in most cases have been referred to me – actually become motivated to cooperate in working toward a preferred goal?"

Other relevant questions are: "How do I achieve that clients themselves take responsibility for their problems and the associated solutions? How do clients ultimately become a 'customer for change'?"

Challenging puberty

The process of finding the answers to these questions is still relatively easy when working with younger children. By their very nature, young children like to cooperate; generally speaking, they tend to be naturally inclined to positive behavior and respond well to compliments and positive attention from guiding adults. Adolescents, however, have all too often a history of disappointment and have perhaps even become accustomed to being approached negatively, all of which results in a lesser positive expectation.

Starving the negative of attention

The Solution Focused approach very quickly breaks down the pattern of negative expectations, simply because the negative behavior is no longer acknowledged. In fact, it's even simpler: the coach just doesn't pay any attention to it. In fact, you as a coach do exactly the opposite: you constantly invite your client to act positively; your focus is only on where progress can be achieved. Young children understand this really fast and very quickly see the benefits for themselves. But with adolescents, this all too often requires a greater investment in energy, time, and attention – both from themselves and from you, the coach.

Preparing for an optimal start

All five different themes of the Mission Possible-program are aimed at raising motivation to an optimal level. In the overview of the steps of Mission Possible, you have already looked a little deeper into this vital topic. You may have noticed that these five themes correspond with the five most important psychological factors involved in creating autonomous motivation. These five factors provide the ground for a resounding 'YES!' to the client's development toward his preferred goal. These are the preconditions for a successful Mission Possible-program in which problems and goals are taken into ownership.

Ownership

From this position of ownership, the client is truly a 'customer for change', because he will take full responsibility for his own developments toward his goal. The steps of the Mission Possible-program are fully aimed at guiding the client to this point of autonomous motivation, thereby opening the way to growing self-confidence and progress from a sense of autonomy, relationship and competence. Therefore, the client is during the entire process in fact independent. When you accurately determine the client's position at the start of his process, he will be able to connect and find the best-fitting interventions to help him to achieve an optimal level of motivation and ensure a successful finish.

Tools for the toolbox

Seven important Solution Focused questions:

1   Asking about change happening before the first session
2   Asking about goals (like 'the miracle question')
3   Asking for more or more in depth ('What else?')
4   Asking for exceptions (when the problem doesn't occur or occurs less)
5   Scaling questions (aimed at progress, motivation, and confidence)
6   Asking for resources (competences, experiences, talents, traits the clients already possesses)
7   Coping questions (in times of crisis)

When do adolescents become 'customers for change'?

It might actually sound a bit strange to use the expression: 'customer' or 'co-expert for change' in the context of finding cooperation with young people. What is meant by this expression, and how do you know whether adolescents with whom you work in fact are or are not 'customers for change'? In order to find answers to these questions, you first have to make a small assessment of five things at the beginning of the first conversation, a five-point checklist:

1   Being motivated to cooperate
2   Experiencing a problem
3   Requesting help
4   Taking ownership
5   Inward orientation and reflecting

You assess these five points to determine whether you and your client can already start working toward a goal or need to perform some other intervention first. For each point, you can distinguish three positions that are named to keep them apart: 'visitor', 'seeker or complainer', and 'customer or co-expert'. These names will probably not immediately arouse your enthusiasm, because they might seem somewhat negative at first glance. But they are not meant to share with your client. They are only meant for you to internally assess the position of the adolescent's motivational platform at that moment. It is a snapshot with no other purpose than to help you connect with your client in the most promising way. This way you ensure the conversation will unfold a lot nicer, without triggering resistance, and through collaboration providing useful information. Just doing what works!

The following is an overview in which this assessment of the motivation platform and the three possible client's motivational categories are made visual, along with the typical characteristics of each position.

The 'customer' or 'co-expert'

Put simply, an adolescent is a consulting 'customer or co-expert for change' when he's ready to fully commit to that change. It means he has come for help and is willing to cooperate with you, the coach, because he realizes to have a problem he wants to solve. He understands that he himself is part of the solution and is willing to take responsibility for this awareness and its consequences.

The 'seeker or complainer'

Then there's the adolescent who appears to come to you for help but is not yet ready and willing to take responsibility for resolution; he belongs

Tools for the toolbox

Motivation platform: preconditions for being a 'customer for change'

	Visitor	*Seeker/complainer*	*Customer/co-expert*
Motivation	No motivation to cooperate	Some motivation to cooperate	Motivation to cooperate
Problem experience	No experience of problem	Experiences a problem	Experiences a problem
Request for help	No request for help	Requests for help or complaints about problem	Requests for help
Ownership	Takes no responsibility for solution	Takes no or just partial responsibility for solution	Takes partial or full responsibility for solution
Orientation	Externalizing (orientation is external)	Orientation is external	Self-reflecting (orientation is internal)

to the category that is called 'seeker' or 'complainer'. He clearly has some experience of having a problem. He usually does want you to help but is not yet ready or able to fully take on responsibility for his part in the problem and finding an acceptable solution. The seeker or complainer tends to place responsibility for the problem, and especially for working on a solution, partially or even completely somewhere else, outside of him. His orientation is one of accusation rather than being self-reflective. You will need to take a different approach to help this client to achieve the sufficient motivation to fully commit to the collaboration.

'Visitor'

The so-called visitor is someone who shows no obvious sign of being motivated and is far away from expressing a request for help, even to the point of being in denial of the fact that there's anything wrong. After all, he's generally been sent by someone else (in authority) and has only come to meet the coach for the sake of appearances and because he is expected to. Compared with other age groups, the 'visitor' tends to be significantly more prevalent among young teenagers and adolescents.

Powerful compliments

Both the visitor and the seeker/complainer respond well to direct compliments ("Great that you came!"), positive appreciation of personality traits ("I'm so glad you mention not to have much time. It shows you don't like to waste your time. Good, nor do I."), and questions about skills (indirect appreciation, such as: "What things are you really good at in school?"). Such questions and compliments are all quite powerful, motivating interventions. The conversation benefits from this positive approach: your client feels invited to look both at himself and at the interaction with you, the coach, in a positive light.

Align and connect

In the end, all this is a playful mixture of objective observation, carefully listening well, connecting, and tempting the client with the exclusive aim of achieving positive cooperation. Sometimes all it takes is walking a step with your client, throwing out a little 'bate to catch a fish' by asking carefully planned questions … Whatever helps to raise the client's cooperation and motivation to embark on a journey toward a preferred goal is put to use. And it will be surprising how much of what is presented actually is potentially useful. Even undesirable behavior, which, in different circumstances, you might not agree on or find intolerable, is most certainly useful as a possible resource to which you can respond with empathy. The feelings and emotions you encounter can be recognized. Seeing and validating the client's underlying good intentions goes a long way. A person who feels heard and seen will most likely open up more.

Asking for the obvious

A useful way of starting the conversation and gaining your client's involvement and cooperation is simply to ask some questions to which the only possible answer is YES. Creating this so-called yes set eases the way to the next stage in the conversation, where the questions may become somewhat more challenging. This way you, as coach, create a positive pattern of expectations on the client's side for the remains of the conversation.

An example of yes set questions

In a calm tempo, the coach asks at least three questions to which the only honest answer would be 'yes'. The effect is generally that, by creating a positive expectation, the chance that the client will relax and cooperate is optimized.

It is important to emphasize that the coach must find questions to which the answer will be affirmative with one hundred percent certainty. If not, this technique fails. This means that the coach needs to ask closed questions, which already include the answer, like these simple examples:

Coach: You're Karen, aren't you?
Karen: Yes. I am.
Coach: And you're 13 years old?
Karen: Yes.
Coach: You're in your second year at your high school?
Karen: Yes. Indeed I am.
Coach: And Mr. Jones will be your class teacher, if I'm correct?
Karen: Yes. You're right.
Coach: Until now, you've had pretty good results – isn't that so?
Karen: Yes. I believe I have.

By ending up with a question about positive results, characteristics, or skills, you create an opportunity to give a compliment:

Coach: That's really great, Karen – getting such good results! You must have worked really hard. Or haven't you? How did you manage to achieve such good results studying?

Giving an indirect compliment can also be effective.

Coach: Mr. Jones tells me you have excellent grades and that you study really hard. Karen, how do your parents feel about your getting such good results at school?

By now, Karen, the client in the above example, has had time to get used to the situation. Moreover, the style of questioning used by her coach has created a more positive expectation of the conversation that will follow. Any resistance on Karen's side, if ever there was any, is therefore already diminished. Resistance is, in most cases, nothing more than fear of the unknown. It is seldom opposed to the situation. Just consider that all behavior, including initial resistance, comes from an intrinsically positive intention, which is why it is possible to use it constructively in building a good coaching relationship. It's even possible to conclude that 'resistance' as such actually doesn't exist. In fact, labeling behavior as 'resistance' is not a useful concept. Since the Solution Focused approach invites you to 'do what works', labeling behavior as negative behavior, based on an unwillingness to cooperate, will harm the relationship between you and your client and only leads you farther away from progress.

> *Coach:* Karen, I see that you're holding back a little about telling me what reasons you have for this meeting. I find that remarkable. Most students who come to talk to me are pretty angry and in quite a hurry to tell me what has happened. I can see you are very well in control of yourself. That can't always be so easy. I have to admit that I can't always control myself when I am angry about something. Can you tell me how you manage to do that so well?

Even if Karen replies with something like "I don't know" or "No idea," the indirect compliment has done its positive work. There's a good chance that Karen now will respond more curiously expecting rather than closed off and resisting. One thing is virtually certain: her expectations about how the conversation will proceed have been positively influenced. The coach sees Karen's initial resistance and chooses to reframe it as a 'little too much' of a positive personality trait; this decision is a valuable and highly constructive tool in the attempt to build a basis of constructive cooperation between coach and client.

A gentle word of warning here: such an intervention should not be used in the event of behavior that you would judge to be destructive or dangerous. It is relevant at this point to stress that physical force of any kind from your client (hitting, kicking, scratching) is never acceptable. The same applies to verbal abuse (swearing, teasing, bullying) and other socially unacceptable behavior (spitting, vandalism, sabotage, taking revenge by abusive posting on social media, etc.). Such behavior goes beyond what is considered here as 'resistance' and should be appropriately addressed and dealt with.

Positions for change: a typology

Here's an excerpt and further explanation of the various characteristics of clients.

The visitor

- has little or no motivation to cooperate (he is all too often sent)
- doesn't feel he has a problem (it's other people who have a problem)
- doesn't have or recognize any need for help (doesn't have any problems)
- doesn't take responsibility for the solution (it's not his problem)
- is externally oriented (it's the others who have to change)

The seeker/complainer

- has at least some motivation to cooperate (he recognizes that there is a problem)
- admits he has a problem (something is troubling him)
- has to some extent a need for help (he wants to stop experiencing the problem)
- doesn't take responsibility for the solution (it's the others who must change; it's their fault, and they should therefor resolve the problem)
- is primarily externally oriented (ignores his own part in the situation)

The customer or co-expert

- is motivated to cooperate (wants to resolve the problem)
- is aware that he has a problem (it's a nuisance)
- asks for help (wants to be helped to find a solution)
- takes responsibility for the solution (understands that he will have to do something in order to make it happen)
- is self-reflecting (is able to look at his own part in the situation)

A case study from school: Martin

Martin enters. From his way of walking, one could not hope for much openness. He drops himself into a chair in the middle of the room and starts rolling a cigarette. "Already in advance for my break," he claims. "Because I suspect I will miss out on most of that one, probably ..." [silence]

Coach: Good afternoon. You're Martin, aren't you?
Martin: Yes.
Coach: Did you come straight out of your classroom?
Martin: Yes.
Coach: And you were sent by your teacher?
Martin: Yes.
Coach: English? That's Mr. Jones, isn't it?
Martin: Yes.
Coach: Well, what can I do for you?
Martin: Yeah, well, how would I know? I had to come here from that (bleep) Mr. Jones, my English teacher, I mean.
Coach: *[Ignoring Martin's bad language]* Okay. And I understand you had some kind of problem together?
Martin: I don't know. He seems to have a problem. He always does. With me, I mean ... *[Martin's anger seems to be changing into something else here. He is showing signs of feeling hurt more than being angry]* If someone (bleep) up, I always get

blamed first. I don't want to go back to class with that man. There's just no talking to him. If I try to explain, all he does is shut me up immediately.

Coach: That sounds pretty annoying, if you feel that always is what happens. I can imagine you're fed up with that. Would you like to share more about it?

Martin: Well, I wouldn't know. I didn't really do anything. Everybody was fooling around. That stupid (bleep) just can't keep order.

Coach: Oh, I see. Are there any moments when Mr. Jones and you *do* see eye to eye?

Martin: Not in class. Only when I see him outside school; then he's a totally different dude. Then he's more or less okay, more relaxed. Actually, then he's quite nice even. But teaching just isn't his best thing, I guess. He's a nervous wreck.

Coach: So, when you meet outside classes, you have a much better understanding with Mr. Jones, you say?

Martin: Yeah, sort of. I met him last weekend on his bike. He has the same brand bike as I do, and he races on weekends. With his brother, he was. We then spent a long time standing around talking and done even a bit of cycling together.

Coach: Oh, how nice. So, you share a hobby? And even the same sort of racing bicycle.

Martin: Yep. He bought it just a few months ago, almost the same month as I did. I saved for it a very long time, from my job at the supermarket. Stocking shelves, you know. He said he found it really awesome, cause it's a really cool bike.

Coach: That is indeed a big achievement. I bet it took a lot of perseverance. I guess it needs a lot of motivation, doesn't it? Great, though, that Mr. Jones recognized that, don't you think so, too?

Martin: Yeah, he was a real nice bloke then.

Coach: I like hearing you say that. I think it's wonderful that you are able to admit to that, in spite of your initial anger toward him in the present situation. It shows me you are able to also see the good things and see past the bad.

Martin: Well, every person has something good. It's not all black and white. So?

Coach: No, I guess you're right in that. Fortunately, I'd say. *[Long pause]*

Coach: What would you think could be done to improve the situation for you in class during Mr. Jones's lessons? It sounds as if there could be some possibilities.

Martin: Yeah, if only he could be as when he is biking.

Coach: Hm. You two really seem to hit it off there. How would we be able to use that for a better cooperation during class hours?

Martin: Yeah *duhhh*. That's a good question. Go for a bike ride to talk about it? It's a bit difficult in the classroom.

Coach: Well? In some other moment?

Martin: *[Looks as if his coach has gone mad]* Wouldn't he think it strange? If I ask now, I mean? I really shouted at the dude just before.

Coach: When we are angry, we all tend to do or say things we regret afterwards. Don't you think he will understand?

Martin: Then you'd want me to make apologies first?

Coach: What do you think? What would you want someone to do if something similar happened to you?

Martin: Yeah, whatever. I was really angry. It was so unfair, you know. But racing our bikes and then talk about it is an idea. I can ask him why he's always picking on me. It could sure help not always being the only one who gets sent off to the principal or to you. I get to learn something too then, and my mom will be getting some peace. Will be a nice change to have her off of my case as well.

Coach: Martin, you already see a lot of benefits. What can you do to make it happen? Which small step can you think of to achieve this?

Martin: Pfff. *[Sticks his cigarette behind his ear]* Lunch break is almost over, huh? Can I still go and see him now? Or do I have to wait until after school hours?

Coach: What would work best for you?

Martin: *[stunned]* Can I decide? Oh. I think I would prefer to go now. Otherwise, it is the whole afternoon hanging over my head. Do you think it's okay to do it now?

Coach: We can ask him, okay.

Martin: ... *[Turns his cap and stands up immediately]* Yes, shall we? *[While standing up simultaneously, he suddenly hesitates]* You know, I think I can manage on my own. I feel it's a little stupid to walk the halls with you. And ... uh, can I first have a quick smoke? Just calming down my nerves a bit?

Coach: Okay, I figure a five-minute break won't hurt. I think you're right about being able to do it on your own. Good luck! Will I hear from you how it went?

[Two hours later in the hallway]

Coach: Hey Martin. And?

Martin: Well, I went to ask, about the biking and he said yes. He came to the hall when he saw me. He did ask what I wanted to talk about. And I immediately said I had the feeling he always has to pick on me when there is trouble and everybody is messing around in class. And I did apologize for my outburst *[Laughs]* You will never guess what he said.

Coach: No, I have absolutely no idea.

Martin: He said he has nothing against me personally. On the contrary, he thinks I'm cool. But he sometimes finds it hard to keep order in our class, since we are such a lively bunch, he said. And he says I'm a natural leader. The others look up to me and listen. And when he addresses me, the rest quiet down more easily.

Coach: Wow, how do you feel about that?

Martin: First I didn't know what to say, but then he said it's actually one of my best qualities. And he said he didn't realize I would feel unfairly treated by his remarks. He promised in future to take better notice and try to handle it in a different way. I think that's really cool of him. I mean, that he admitted he was wrong.

Coach: What does that mean to you, Martin?

Martin: Well, wow, just a lot. I don't feel angry any longer. I understand better now. It also feels, somehow, like having received a huge compliment.

Coach: That's fantastic, Martin. You're very generous.

Martin: What on earth does that mean? I know that word only from my mum, when she says I put too many chocolate sprinkles on my bread.

Coach: *[Laughing]* It means you sometimes may have a big mouth, but probably your heart is even bigger.

Martin: *[Stands up with a big grin on his face]* Well, don't tell anyone.

Coach: *Tell what? I don't know what you're talking about. See you, Martin, and have a nice evening.*

This story about Martin could easily give the impression that all problems get resolved in one session or conversation. The reality is usually different, but in this case, Martin is indeed a good-hearted, generous young man. He clearly likes people and likes equally to get them involved, to include them, qualities that the coach in this case study wisely makes good use of.

Notice, too, how this coach cleverly asks Martin to switch perspectives – "What would *you* do if you were … ?" – to look at the situation as if he were the teacher. This type of questioning can be highly effective with young people who may all too easily get stuck in their own perspective.

Similar questions include:

- "How do you think your friends would handle this situation?"
- "How does that affect you?"
- "How do you feel about it?"

Such questions that help to show that there is more than just the client's point of view also serve to open up the way to new, unforeseen solutions. The questions should be formulated so that the client perceives that *his* point of view is both respected and accepted – which avoids the deadlock around who is right. It is essential to be aware of avoiding the 'who is right' issue, as that is irrelevant in the Solution Focused approach.

Building a platform for cooperation

The key to success in the client–coach relationship is building a *connection*: a mutually respectful conversation between equals.

That's not always easy; after all, since you have a job to do and often are older, there's an apparent initial inequality. However, this can, to some extent, be mitigated by awareness of one's attitude and being flexible in giving priority to the client and *his* process. Simply being *aware* of any existing judgment (about the client and his situation) helps to set it aside for later – or not at all! – and should be considered inherent to correct Solution Focused practice.

A personal note, which may be valid for some coaches, concerns your facial expression. I personally am very open and equally expressive, so I have a long-term learning process around this important aspect, since I am simply unable to hide what I think or feel! Let me share what I have so far discovered to be very useful: keeping a positive frame of mind. Always looking at matters from a positive point of view certainly helps avoid anything but a favorable judgment! And that positive judgment serves, in turn, to strengthen the bond with your client in an utterly creative process of mutual discovery.

Instant creativity

Martin's story shows this need for an in-the-moment creative approach. This requires not only a positive Solution Focused attitude from you, which I will discuss in a separate chapter later in this book, but also knowledge of the effects of an intervention. Every question you ask is a conscious choice with a predetermined goal. For those who do not yet have much experience with the Solution Focused approach and the effect of the various interventions, I will give an overview of possible interventions that suit the different positions in 'client typology'. It should be noted that it is also quite possible that someone can be in more than one position at the same time.

Waiting to jump to conclusions

For example, Martin, in the above story, is a 'visitor' at first glance. Martin is sent by his teacher, Mr. Jones, to go and see the coach. He is angry and seems at first to have little good expectations of the conversation ahead. He even expresses that negative expectation at some point. But because the coach does not respond to this and quietly examines what is important to Martin specifically, it soon becomes clear that Martin is indeed experiencing a problem. He complains about the, in his opinion, unfair behavior of the teacher and shares how he is annoyed by it. Martin therefore has an interest to change. And that becomes clearly evident in this conversation. An assessment of the client's position is therefore not done in five seconds. It is a process of objective observation during the whole conversation until it can be established that the position of the 'customer' for change has been reached. From that moment on, Martin is a co-expert in working on a workable solution.

Interventions for each position

The visitor

- Acquire a mandate for cooperation from your client by connecting and building trust, and find out who or what is important for him.
- Recognize and acknowledge his feelings and position, and give compliments (for what is already there).
- Inquire with your client about the reasons of the person that referred him to you. Ask about your client's own vision on the matter. ("What do you think of the situation yourself? How do you see this?")

The complainer

- Acquire a mandate for cooperation by connecting, acknowledging feelings, and complimenting good traits.
- Translate your client's complaints into needs or wishes.
- Ask questions about relationships (with other people, with previously found solutions in similar situations, etc.).
- Ask questions about exceptions to the problem: "What was different in that particular situation, when the problem did not occur?"

The customer or co-expert

- Explore the preferred future and goals together.
- Clarify the discovered goals by asking to be more specific.
- Identify all available resources (both internal and external).
- Cooperatively determine feasible steps in the desired direction and make a plan.

Carefully building connection and trust is key by setting up a coaching climate in which you and your client are equal discussion partners. That sometimes can be a challenging task that requires mostly patience and a totally open 'beginner' attitude. Here you are asked to be flexible and to subordinate yourself and to be available to the client's process. Postponing or, if it is present, just parking your usually immediately present opinions on the situation is a prerequisite. For those who, like me, have an expressive face, this is a learning process for the longer term. What has proven to be a great tool in my experience is to adopt a positive attitude. If you always first look with a positive eye, the judgment is usually also positive. And a positive judgment can again be put to use as a means to establish the optimal motivation of the 'customer or co-expert relationship' of your coachee (Berg, I.K. & de Jong, P., 2001, *Interviewing for solutions; De Kracht van Oplossingen*).

A case study from school: John

Next to the schoolyard, there's a small field where the children can play football after classes.

John has just kicked the ball and has broken a window. The automatic alarm service has passed on a message to the teacher on duty – Mr. Smith – who is now standing in the schoolyard with the ball in his hand. John is standing next to him as they together inspect the damage. John is expecting a severe reprimand, but Mr. Smith asks him: "Do I understand correctly that you were over on the other side of the field, John? And you kicked the ball from way over there? Amazing! How come you haven't yet been scouted for the national team, John? How did you manage to do it, kicking the ball with such power all across that enormous distance?"

John, rather taken aback by the teacher's compliments in the questions, answers: "Well, yes, we were playing over there, and the ball somehow landed in the yard. I just wanted to kick it back onto the football field."

Mr. Smith:	Aha! So, if I understand you correctly, the ball rolled into the yard while playing, and you went over there and kicked it back? From the yard?
John:	Yes, sir.
Mr. Smith:	Thank you for being honest with me, John. I appreciate that. And what does this mean?
John:	Uuh … well, we're not allowed to play football in the yard.
Mr. Smith:	Yes … and how do you think we're going to fix things now, John?
John:	I'll get Mike to help me clear up the broken glass, sir. Will I be punished?

Pattern-breaking surprise

Naturally John's teacher is not happy about being disturbed on his evening off, just as he isn't happy about the damage to the window and the work involved in emergency repairs. But importantly, he manages to mask any negative feelings he might have with a sauce of admiration for the mighty performance of a good shot. It is an approach that takes John by surprise. This sort of pattern-breaking intervention is an unusual approach that helps immensely to pave the way for positive communication.

Truth as the easiest way

The advantage of Mr. Smith's surprising approach is that John now feels invited to be honest about what happened. Or maybe on the spur of the moment, it was just too complicated for John to quickly produce a credible alternative story rather than telling the truth. It does not matter what the reason is; it is important that by breaking the pattern of negative expectations, Mr. Smith creates an opening for a more creative and fruitful communication. This in turn saves a lot of time and trouble (dealing with what's past and what's wrong) and enables speedy decisions and action to solve the problem.

Melting resistance

Moreover, Mr. Smith's style invites John to take responsibility for what has happened and – simply – to move forward, fixing what needs to be fixed. John's question about the consequences of the incident is, of course, easy to understand. Rules are rules, and there are usually penalties for violating them. However, in the light of John's responses, it's reasonable to assume that no punishment is required for John to have learned his lesson. The fact that he receives a compliment for how quickly he will take action indicates that he has already learned what he needs to learn from this incident. If, however, John does have to receive a penalty to not create a precedent, he will now be able to accept it without much resistance.

Structure follows process

Besides that, reaching a point at which the client becomes aware of his autonomous motivation for taking steps toward change, the 'customer position' can also be seen as a preparation step. But it would be a mistake to assume that the program must be carried out in chronological order. Like Kids'Skills, Mission Possible is a fluid system, in essence a structure without content. Throughout the program, the content always takes precedence over the structure. In other words, steps are taken at the moment that they are relevant. The program follows the process instead of dictating it.

Like magic

It is therefore not a cast-iron beam structure in which only the concrete for the walls, floors, and ceilings of the building has yet to be poured. Much more than that, it is like the moving stairwells of Harry Potter's magical school, Hogwarts, which flexibly adjust to the needs and possibilities of the moment, making connections depending on who is on the stairs and what the purpose of their journey is.

Mix and match!

Steps can be mixed up, skipped, repeated, and sometimes even used to the advantage of, and incorporated in, another step. For example, step 2 (benefits) and 7 (scaling) can be excellently used to make step 0. Or step 1 (goal) and step 6 (resources) can be integrated in step 7 (scaling). In fact, everything can be used in the way it works best at that specific moment. Remember rule 1 of the Solution Focused approach: Do what works!

Chapter 3

Getting clear about the goal

Before a Mission Possible process can start at step 1, the adolescent client must have made the decision to work on a solution to his problems or toward a chosen goal. A certain amount of structured research is required in order to arrive at the correct description of the solution. The first step of the Mission Possible-program is therefore designed with this in mind: to determine the goal accurately. The Mission Possible workbook uses questions to guide the adolescent step by step toward a concrete description of the goal (solution) he's working toward.

Starting with a dream

With step 1, the workbook helps uncover the underlying dreams and needs of the client; this step is especially significant, since at this early stage in the process, such dreams and needs are generally present only at an unconscious level. Or, when consciously present, they are already dismissed as unreachable.

Valuable preparation

In order to gain a truly clear picture of the goal, a number of preconditions have to be met. These are the first two themes of the Mission Possible-program, which, as you have seen before, are more or less equal to the first two factors of autonomous motivation. These themes include steps 0, 1, 2, and the subsequent steps 7 and 11.

Step 1: The goal

Introduction to step 1

In the very first version of the Mission Possible-program, as published in 2010, step 1 was still based on the originally developed program by Ben Furman and on the concept of the dream, an ideal and perfect future. This dreamed-up perfect future was the starting point, the basis for the determination of the goal for the Mission Possible-program. However, several studies into the effects of the Solution Focused approach and my own experiences have shown that this principle of a perfect future can actually counteract progress.

Triggering the negative

I have also observed much confirmation of this idea in my practice. This is why, in this revised edition of the Mission Possible-program, this first step has been redesigned into what already was my practice for some time: the principle of an ideal dream of the future gradually has been abandoned. The ideal future does not exist and will most likely never be achieved. That is a fact of life. After all, adversity is an inherent part of our lives. In fact, children who never experience adversity are rarely successful in later life, simply because they have not learned to deal with that part of reality.

A future in which the current problem does not exist

It does justice to our human reality to have a more realistic view instead of focusing on an unachievable ideal image. Embracing human imperfection and looking at what is desired from this perspective enhances the chance to overcome adversity. The principle of a preferred future based on the no-longer-existing problem is the new starting point. And when the problem in fact turns out to be a limitation or handicap, which in itself is unsolvable, at least acceptance of this limitation, or solving the problems around the limitation, can be a very achievable goal. Cooperative research into the possibilities within this existing limitation can lead to improvement of the problems around it.

With this revision of step 1 of the Mission Possible-program, it has become a more progress-focused rather than Solution Focused approach, no longer focused on achieving a pre-idealized goal, but focused on development and growth in a preferred direction.

> *"A goal without an actual agreement to take action is nothing more than a dream."*

Based on the current situation, which has room for improvement, you focus directly on the preferred situation, the future in which the problem is solved or at least improved. Visualizing this preferred situation over, for example, a few months, a year, or even longer, is the foundation of the chosen goal for the Mission Possible-program. With a clear and specific destination, it is indeed a Mission Possible. This preferred future is a necessary basis for identifying goals.

To determine what actions are needed to grow toward a new situation, a clear and specified picture of the desired change is needed as a starting point. When we describe this in detail, it becomes clear what needs to be done and what can be learned or improved in order to realize it.

Describing the preferred future

Many young people have difficulty in describing their desired or preferred future. At that age, they're all too often occupied with discovering who they are and what their place is in the world; many are simply busy with living in the here and now, and that's already quite a task!

Changing perspective

The question of how they would like their future to look in a year, for example, does not always provide a clear answer. "I do not know" is the dreaded response for any novice coach, who may not have the experience yet and has few questions ready. If the first answer does not immediately provide clarity, it may help to suggest that the answer to that question be explored together. This can be done, for example, by asking the young client if he would like to describe a vivid picture of himself, for example over about a year or other useful time frame. For this purpose, the typically Solution Focused miracle-questions are a perfect choice.

> "Imagine that you are very satisfied with your life in a few years' time. You feel that everything is going well, and you are going through a beautiful time in your life … How would that look for you? How would you feel? What would you do, for example? Where would you live? And what would you study, or what profession would you have?"

Useful fantasy

At this stage, it does not matter whether the answers that are given from the current perspective are completely realistic. Someone may want to be a famous rapper or want to have his own talk show. It is about finding out what the adolescent finds important in his life, what he finds himself enthusiastic about – as long as this dreamed future perspective only gives energy instead of triggering limiting beliefs.

A case study from practice: Josh and Marsha continuation

It's time to see how Josh is getting on, the young man whom you met earlier in this book because of how he mistreated his younger sister, Marsha. Now Josh is having a meeting alone with the coach – in this case, me – without his mother Inez or Marsha present. Marsha has made it clear that for the time being, she doesn't want to meet with me personally but would prefer to be supported by email. She explains that the presence of her brother intimidates her so that she doesn't dare be forthcoming during a meeting together with Josh.

I talk to Josh about his sister's reticence and, without me specifically asking him, he admits that he would use anything that she said during a coaching session together in order to bully her later.

Acting out of boredom

I ask him: "What benefits would you have, Josh, bullying Marsha in this way, using information she's given at such a meeting?"

Josh immediately understands what I mean and replies that he does it so as to avoid feeling bored or annoyed. "It's a game, a sort of competition," he adds. He goes on to admit that he *does* understand that it is painful for her, and that *does* bother him at a deeper level.

We continue talking for a while about this issue of boredom and how this leads to annoyance and bullying.

At a certain moment, he changes the subject. Josh tells me that he enjoys working with his hands, like fixing scooters and bikes. These days, he spends a lot of time at the computer, something he also enjoys. Nevertheless, it clearly doesn't help to counteract the boredom that constantly gnaws at him.

What would your future look like in, say ...

I then ask him: "How would you like your future life to look in, let's say, two years' time, Josh?"

At first, he has difficulty in answering but then quickly says, "Well, one thing I know is that I hope I won't be living at home anymore."

My next question: "What would you like to see happen instead, Josh?" Immediately, this unleashes a series of answers that seem to come from nowhere. It's as if he's not thinking any longer. Rather, there seems to be a flow of awareness that comes from a deeper place within him. It's precisely the place where authentic answers are usually to be found.

"Perhaps I'd like a job at a cycle repair shop," he says. "When things are uncomfortable at home, I like to go out to the shed and fix my bike. That calms me down. Actually, it would be really great if I could work with other boys in a workshop where lots of people drop in."

Clearly, Josh enjoys having people around him. He goes on to explain, "It's why I go after my sister when I'm bored."

We make an agreement that he's going to think further about this new insight when he's back home. Also, he's going to make a list of all the skills he's going to need in order to get such a job. The next time we meet, we'll then look at the list together and see what skills he already has developed. The other items can then serve as goals for what Josh still needs to learn and that he can work at acquiring.

Straight away, Josh mentions a number of things that he would have to be able to do in order to get such a job. And he immediately adds, "Yes, but those I can easily do already."

There's a new lightness in his step as he walks toward the door, quite different from the otherwise wearisome way he usually drags his feet. Before he closes the door behind him, he turns and gives me a broad grin. His baseball cap is back to front so that I can now see his eyes clearly for the first time.

This meeting with Josh is marked by an increasing openness in the communication. He is more at ease and seems to be starting to accept, slowly but surely, that the current situation as he now experiences it is not destined to stay like this forever. He starts allowing himself to dream more and to look at what is inside him that wants to come out. More and more pieces of the puzzle that is known as 'Josh' start presenting themselves. He starts to recognize that this is who he really is, and *that* catches his interest to explore and discover more fully.

As he proceeds on this path of self-discovery and revelation, his confidence grows in the truth that it's all right for him to be who he is. The small openings in his defensive mask make me increasingly fond of this apparently cheerful, optimistic, and witty young man – a totally different personality from the way he presented himself in the beginning.

A case study from practice: George

Due to serious circumstances in his family, 16-year-old George has had to repeat a year at school. However, his grades are too low even this second time for him to be able to continue his education at this school. He finds himself now confronted with the need to start different studies at a new school with lower requirements – and ultimately a lower level of education. George is quite intelligent and experiences this threatening switch of schools as a considerable blow to his self-esteem. Even though it was impossible for him to do anything about the circumstances that made successfully studying so difficult for him, he feels nevertheless deeply ashamed of what he sees as his personal failure. He gets depressed and loses all faith in creating a favorable future for himself. He even says that he believes that he is cursed in some way. He calls it a 'jinx' or 'evil eye' that makes being lucky impossible for him.

Almost losing hope

Because this most recent negative experience has reduced his motivation even further, he's lost any idea of what he should do and what direction of study he should now choose.

He is even unsure as to whether he actually wants to remain in school and thinks it might be better to stop his formal education and simply start looking for work. But a future of low-paid, unskilled jobs – because he has not graduated and would be leaving school without a diploma – seems very unattractive to him. He has at this moment absolutely no idea what his direction for his future should be. "Everything I do always fails anyway," he says.

Discovering George's special talent

As we together take a look at everything he enjoys doing and the things that are important to him, a number of issues quickly get clearer for George. For example, he very much enjoys being with his friends and – most important – he enjoys cooking dinners for them. He loves working in the kitchen and has discovered his highly developed sense of taste and smell. It's even got to the point that when he and his friends get together, they sometimes organize blindfolded smelling and tasting competitions. He's become very popular with this characteristic trait and is even jokingly referred to as 'George the Nose'.

Secret dream

At the same time as he tells me this with a certain reluctance, it's clear that he's also rather proud of it.

When I ask him where he sees himself in a year's time, he's unable to answer. But in, say, five years' time, he *does* have an answer. "I'd be very happy to have a good job in a restaurant kitchen," he says. Apparently, he has a secret dream to become a famous chef like Jamie Oliver, but at the same time, he immediately sabotages himself by saying that he doesn't believe he can turn his dream into a reality.

Jamie Oliver, whose shows he often watches on 24Kitchen, is clearly a hero for George.

I: What do you think you'd have to change, George, to make your dream come true?

George: No idea ... but it doesn't matter, because there's no way I can get there.

Interestingly enough, George is perfectly capable of outlining two options for 'anyone else' who would want to pursue such a goal:

George: Y'know, there are plenty of training courses for chefs to be, or they could go straight away and work in a kitchen and take part-time courses – learning on the job ...

Possibilities for others

We talk about the various advantages of these two possibilities. Of course, these are advantages for 'anyone else', that is, not for George. It soon becomes clear that full-time study ensures the best possibilities to develop the skills needed to reach his desired career level. Still, the option of learning on the job has the advantage that it's immediately possible to earn a salary and be self-supporting, an option that would be a of great advantage to him.

Internalizing new ideas

While George compares the possibilities offered by both options, it's clear that he is getting more enthusiastic for talking about these newly discovered opportunities. As the conversation proceeds, he gradually talks less about the subject and more about himself as a candidate for such a possible process. He agrees with me that he will ask his mentor at school to help him find out about possible scholarships that would enable him to follow a full-time training course.

New beginnings

At the next meeting, George announces that he has kept his agreement and has spoken with his mentor, who helped him discover that a scholarship is indeed available ... and that he has decided to sign up for the special restaurant chef's training. With his current school qualifications, he could immediately start the first year of this professional three-year training.

The goal that brings the preferred future closer

A clear picture of the better future is important for much more than just identifying a goal to work toward. A clear image of a future in which the problem no longer seems to exist, or at least has been significantly improved, helps people to stay optimistic about the future. A positive, optimistic view helps a client to change a fixed mindset into a growth-mindset. It prevents the loss of hope, an important characteristic of a state of depression.

People who feel depressed often miss a positive view of the future – or at least there's the *sense* that such a perspective is missing. Rediscovering a positive, possible future is one of the greatest advantages of Solution Focused work. Slowly but surely, the client regains his self-confidence as he looks more closely at new possibilities that gradually reveal themselves. And it creates space for new creative insights and alternatives that previously were overlooked.

When you ask about your client's hopes and expectations, you express an inherent degree of respect for your client. After all, you *ask* questions and in no way *tell* your client how he should live his life, a sort of approach most adolescents are pretty allergic to! Such an open style of questioning goes beyond simple honest interest for the direction in which the adolescent chooses to develop – it expresses the fundamental equality in the relationship between coach and client, the two 'players' in this important game of discovery. Moreover, such questions invite a creative cooperation in which the client experiences little (or no!) resistance to answering.

A case study from practice: Samantha

Samantha, an 18-year-old girl, comes to see me after being advised by her school mentor. She failed several of her pre-exams and presents herself with a sad mood. The school mentor, who contacted me before, claims that she lately shows a decreasing interest in her studies and has unexpectedly poor academic performance. Her parents have told him she also is very irritable over seemingly trivial issues. She suffers from anger outbursts and crying spells. One of her best friends also expressed her concern for Samantha, because Samantha expressed feelings of guilt and worthlessness in more than one of their conversations. With the mentor, Samantha discussed suffering from sleep deprivation, experiencing reduced appetite, and having difficulty being attentive and concentrating at school.

Tools for the toolbox

A circle technique

How does it work?

Hang a flip chart or large sheet of paper on the wall and draw two big circles on it, an inner circle and an outer circle (like a traffic sign with an edge). The inner circle represents what has already been achieved (what is already going well). The outer circle represents what still needs to be achieved or what can be improved. Use a marker and ask your client to write down what has already been achieved in the inner circle. Do the same with what still needs to be achieved, but then let him write this on sticky notes instead, and ask him to paste them into the outer circle. This last part can be used as a way of scaling: the closer to the inner circle, the closer the goal already is.

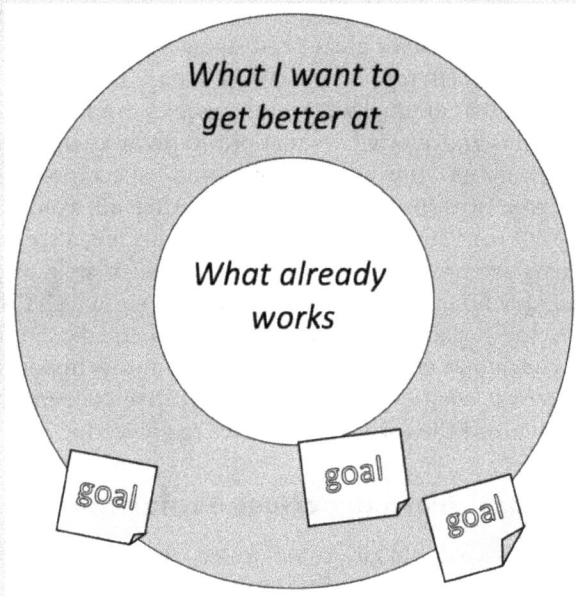

Figure 3.1

Step by step

1   Draw both circles on a large sheet of paper or board.
2   Ask your client what he already has achieved or what he is satisfied or is proud of, and ask him to write this directly in the inner circle. Try to fill this

inner circle as much as possible. This is a way of resourcing and establishing self-confidence for your client.

3   Ask the young client to write on separate sticky notes (max. three) what he still needs to achieve or improve, and ask him to paste them in the outer circle.

4   Ask the young person to choose a small step forward and write down how he wants to achieve it.

5   Ask the client to move the note toward the inner circle as the goal approaches. Once the goal has been achieved, it can be written directly into the inner circle. This is a way of scaling progress.

Variation

The circle can also be divided into segments. For example: one segment for school and one for at home.

Using the circle technique while working with a group

1   Use one set of circles for the entire group, or form little subgroups, each with its own set of circles.

2   The group members write directly in the inner circle what they have already achieved, what they are satisfied with, and what does not have to be changed. What they still want to achieve, they write on notes that they can stick in the outer circle.

3   The circle can also be divided into segments for subgoals and/or focus areas. For example: on the left, topics related to the functioning of the individual, and on the right, subjects that relate to the functioning of the group – or, for example; different perspectives or performance fields or a segment for each individual.

The advantages of the circle technique

1   The technique is simple and goal oriented. The focus is on the essential: making progress in the desired direction.

2   Young people are often pleasantly surprised about what's already working well.

Close to the exit

Samantha sits down in a chair nearest to the door. Before I get a chance to make her feel comfortable and offer her a cup a tea, she starts complaining that she is often unable to remember what was taught in the classroom, as well as what she was reading. She seems very disturbed and agitated when speaking. She says nothing seems to stick in her head these days, at least not longer than a few moments. I ask her if there's anything else she would like to talk about before we start looking at her issues.

What's to gain here?

Samantha: Yes, I would like to know a bit more about what it is you do, and how that can benefit me?

Coach: Fair enough. I can imagine it is nice to know what is in it for you before committing to anything. Well, I work as a Solution Focused therapist and coach. That means I use an approach that focuses on helping clients construct solutions instead of working on solving problems. It means that I like to talk about the things you want instead of talking about things you want to get rid of. How do you feel about that?

Samantha: That certainly sounds better than talking about my problems.

A future without problems

Coach: Good. It doesn't mean we are going to ignore your problems. It just means we will spend most of our time together looking at what you would like them to change into. What would you like to see happen instead of your problems?

Samantha: That's easy to answer. I'd truly like to feel less pressure from my mother to perform better at my studies. She makes me feel I'm an absolute failure. I seem to be unable to please her, whatever I try. She's just never satisfied. If I can't succeed at my exams, I feel it's better to die rather than to fail her high expectations. Not that I ever did attempt suicide or something. It's nothing like that, but I feel very guilty that I'm unable to fulfill my parents' dreams. *[Now pausing for a while] [Sigh …]* I admit, it does cross my mind every now and then. That is … when I feel really down and just want it all to stop. The pressure and the nagging, I mean. It's like it always goes on, even when I'm alone. I hear this voice, nagging in my head, saying I'm not good enough, not trying and working hard enough, not being smart enough … You know, like that, always.

Taking all the necessary time to vent

I listen to her attentively and with compassion while she talks about her concerns. She looks so anxious and worried. The detailed information she gives about her problems and experiences really paints a clear picture of a young woman that can't cope with the amount of pressure she is under. And she is very aware of it. As I listen and validate her feelings and concerns, this brings some positive change in Samantha, as she feels seen and heard. We sit together and discuss her future goals. Her goals are very clear, and I notice my growing admiration for her.

Clear goals

Samantha: Pass my exams, get my diploma, and go to a good university to do my master's and PhD, maybe even abroad. Then I will be able to find a good job as a lawyer and make my parents proud.

I compliment Samantha for having already taken such a significant step as thinking about her future goals in such detail. Though she seems to feel a little more hopeful, she doesn't yet have a clear vision about how to achieve this preferred future. The goals still seem so unattainable and far away. We agree to take a look at this together. I draw a big circle and an even bigger one around it, a little bit like a traffic sign.

Drawing circles

I hand Samantha a marker and invite her to write everything she can think of that at present is going well in her life in the circle in the middle. She seems to hesitate, but following my instruction, she stands up and walks to the whiteboard and writes down: *I passed two of my exams.*

Coach: Wonderful. What more can you think of?
Samantha: *[Writes again] I had a B for a big test last week.*
Coach: Great. What more is working well for you at the moment?
Samantha: "I am a loyal friend".
Coach: Wow. Fantastic! Write it down.
Samantha: *[Now giggling]* This is fun. I also am class eldest and doing a good job at that. My fellow students appreciate me. I'm tidy. I keep to my commitments. I'm responsible. I'm pretty serious, but I also like to have fun sometimes.

She turns and looks at me, laughing. A completely different, much lighter atmosphere arises. It seems as if she's now just getting warmed up. One by one, her newly discovered traits, talents, achievements, and experiences are filling the inner circle until it is almost entirely full. Then she stops and looks at me.

Samantha: What's the outer circle for?
Coach: Good question. That circle is for everything you would like to get better at. But instead of writing that directly on the paper in the circle, I'd like to ask you to write these things on a yellow sticky note.

Choosing a goal

Coach: Samantha, earlier in our conversation, you talked about identifying three major goals: managing your stress level, enhancing
your concentration, and preparing well for your exams. That
makes three sticky notes, with one goal on each sticker. Where
in the circle would you place these three goals? Outside the
circle, just on the outer edge, or in the middle, or even almost on
the edge of the inner circle? Use it as a scaling tool. The nearer
to the inner circle, the better it already is working for you.

Samantha places her three sticky notes in the outer circle. 'Managing
her stress level' she places on the outer edge of the outer circle.

Samantha: I feel I don't know how to do this, and I really want to get
better at it. Learn skills, I mean.

The other two she places halfway into the outer circle.

Samantha: Well, I already made a plan with my mentor to prepare for
my new exams, and I started preparing already. So I guess
I'm halfway there. And my concentration level is better when
I get enough sleep and when I start on time. Also, I have discovered that when I take more time to relax, my concentration level also goes up. I want to take time off to relax so I
can concentrate better. It's just that I feel so guilty when I do.

Identifying what already works well

Coach: Wow, Sam! That is really fabulous. Two of your goals you've
already started to work on, and you are seeing some results.
And how about your first goal, managing your stress level?
It seems that you have already taken some actions there too.
Samantha: Oh, you're right. That actually has much to do with me
getting better at concentrating. I didn't see that before.
Coach: You worked very hard today, and you are showing excellent motivation and insight. I'm very pleased with the
results. How about you? How do you feel about what we
discussed today?
Samantha: Well, I had no idea I was already on my way to get better.
I'm quite surprised. I feel much better already.
Coach: What would you say if we zoom in on your goals a bit
more next time? Then we can see what is in there. We can
find out if you already have skills and other resources that
can help you to achieve your goals more easily, and we can
have a look at what still needs to be done. Then we can
make a detailed plan.

Samantha: That seems logical to me. Yes, please. I'd like that.
Coach: Great. That's settled then. See you next week, same time.

Where to start

To explore a preferred future, it doesn't make much of a difference whether you and your client start the Mission Possible-program based on the desire to achieve something (a clear future perspective) or whether you want to solve a problem in the here and now. At the most, you might ask some different questions. In both cases, it is an important and powerful moment in the process, where you as a coach can really help your young client to gain more insight into his current situation, as well as into how he would like to see it changed. As soon as he has found the answer to these questions, he will know better where to focus his energy. Since it is often difficult for young people to look beyond their limiting beliefs, you have at this point the task to explore more in depth. In this way, you help your client to explore an alternative future, to set specific goals, and to clarify them. Just asking the question 'how do you see your future?' will rarely be enough. At this point in the process, it is always necessary to keep asking questions to get as clear and as detailed a picture as possible.

Looking for a solution

If your client shares his problem, the following questions can help to evoke a more detailed image of his preferred future:

- What would you like to see happen instead of your problem?
- What would it look like if this problem no longer existed?
- What would be better for you if your problem were solved?
- What would have changed? And what would be indications of such change?
- What would other people notice that has changed?

Setting a goal for the future

If your client wants to set and achieve a goal in the future that is not directly based on an existing problem in the present situation, you can use more general questions, as the following examples show:

- What does your future look like? What dreams or expectations do you foster?
- What would you like to achieve in the future?
- How do you want your current situation to change?
- And how would you notice that you have achieved this?
- Imagine that we are here now in six months or a year: you are doing really well. What do you tell me that is happening for you? What are you doing? What did you achieve?

Persist to explore

In short, you keep asking questions until you have a detailed description of the desired situation in the future. Your main focus is that you receive as many answers as possible to describe your client's preferred future. It may be evident that such descriptions will not always come in a positive package. Your client might experience some difficulty to immediately let go of his negative expectations or limiting beliefs. If his answer comes in a negative description, such as the nonexistence or stopping of his problem, you can help him reframe and translate this positively in your summary. You can also help clarify vague or general answers with thorough and more in-depth questioning. For example, "I no longer want to be unhappy" can be reframed as: "So you want to be happier. What does your being happier look like?"

Adapting your language to your client's

By using his own words as much as possible when you reframe positively and ask further questions, you help your client to describe his desired situation in a concrete and positive way. For example, he can say things like: "I feel cheerful because no one is thinking about doing things I don't like anymore" or "I feel cheerful because we don't ignore each other." The future is often described as the lack of things that bother your client in the current situation. "No one is whining at me or on my case all the time" can be translated into "Everybody now leaves me alone and in peace." And the phrase "We don't ignore each other" can be translated as "We pay attention to each other." This can be processed in the subsequent conversation. For example: "And now that you are paying attention to each other, do you feel a lot happier in their company?" In this way, you help the client to shape his preferred future in detail in positive language.

Going slow in the beginning

It takes your time, effort, and genuine interest to get such a clear picture from your client, especially if you want it to be lively and richly detailed. The question about the future often provides the same kind of answer during the first moments of your interview. Something that will sound similar to "I wouldn't know" or "I've no idea." This indeed can be frustrating, but it certainly doesn't need to be the end of your conversation. In such a case, it is advisable to be a little more persistent and investigative. Just take your time, keep breathing, and continue to ask questions to help the client go deeper into drawing a detailed picture of his preferred future. And in case you run out of options, there's always this set of questions to help you through those awkward moments: "What else? What more can you tell me? Tell me more."

A case study from practice: Ron

Coach: How would your life look in, say, five years' time, Ron?

Ron: I don't know. I absolutely wouldn't know.

Coach: Of course, I understand that it's difficult to give an answer. But just imagine for a moment – here you are, five years from today, totally content with your life in this moment. You're having a great time … Wouldn't that be something? What sort of things would you be doing? What would be happening?

Ron: Well … then I guess I'd probably like to be doing something with music. I mean, I already play the guitar, and I really enjoy that a lot. Who knows, I might even play in my own band.

Coach: Oh wow! That sounds really interesting, Ron. What style of music would you be playing with your band?

Ron: Well, I actually like a whole range of different sorts of music. But when I'm playing, I prefer to play ballads – a sort of blues. I've often composed my own songs and have written the lyrics myself. I can express my feelings a little that way.

Coach: Could you tell me what it is you would be writing about in five years' time, Ron? And how would you go about writing those texts?

Ron: What attracts me most is the idea of writing together with a group or with just one good friend. I'd like to have my own place where we could practice … and there'd probably also be a small recording studio, yes, that'd be perfect! Hmmm, the songs would be about … well, I'm not sure right now. Probably about everything and anything, I guess. Oh yes, about love, of course, right? Aren't most songs about love anyway?

Coach: Well, well … that all sounds very professional and is a wonderful vision of your future. Listening to you just now, I had the feeling that you are already well on your way to creating it.

Ron: Oh, what do you mean?

Coach: Well, you've told me that you already play the guitar. You've obviously got some musical talent. You tell me that you've already written some songs and lyrics … All this seems like a pretty good start, I think.

Ron: Uh, yes, maybe … when you put it like that, yes. The only thing is that there are so many people who want to get into music.

Coach: *[Purposely ignoring the negative remark]* Could you tell me more about your future as a musician in five years' time? I mean, where would I be able to find you? Where can I listen to your music or visit your concert?

Ron: Hmm … If I really start dreaming about it all, then I know I want to travel a LOT. I wouldn't want to always stay in the same place – I don't think so. I think I'd then meet loads of interesting people and, oh yes, I'd get to know some other cultures. That'd be *really* interesting, especially from a musical perspective. I really love old American blues and old-style bluegrass very much. Do you know that? It's from the early fifties. It's fun! I'd like to be playing as often as I could with other musicians, in the studio or, even better, live on tour. For that, I'd first have to get pretty good. Maybe even study music academically for a while ... Ah, and I know, there's not much financial gain in playing such music, but, as long as I can play and enjoy myself, that's all that matters to me.

Fantasy opens up new possibilities

It would be incorrect to just assume that Ron, the young man from the previous conversation, will go on to become a musician; that would depend on numerous factors. But the simple fact that he's able to start forming a picture of an alternative future for himself is what's important and that is sufficiently attractive for him to be willing to invest in the necessary steps to bring it within his reach. It is interesting to notice that Ron becomes aware – as he elaborates on his dream – of the fact that he's already qualified to some degree to turn this dream into a reality. In other words, that part of his dream already *has* been realized. For Ron, this is an important insight that he can build on, make progress, and create successes with his Mission Possible-program. It's as if all of a sudden, out of nowhere, a positive vision of his possibilities emerges, and he discovers his passion and preferences.

Ron discovers all of this because he's encouraged to use his fantasy. The creative questioning by his coach offers him to access his own unlimited imagination.

In this example, the coach starts the interview with the question: "What will your life look like, say, in five years' time?" And with a little help, Ron overcomes his initial reluctance to go into this imaginary world. However, if Ron had found it more difficult to imagine this future situation, there are other ways of asking the question.

Alternative I

Coach: Imagine that today's the day that five years have passed since we first met. How do you see yourself? Where are you now, Ron? Aha – you're smiling, you look really happy! What's happened? What's changed for you that you look so radiant and happy? Keep imagining it and describe it for me in the present tense as if it were really happening right now.

Just asking "What would be different in the future?" out of the blue makes it harder for your client to provide much of an answer. However, you can increase the chance of a comprehensive and detailed answer by asking the question with more imagination and some acting. By introducing the question with an outline of a possible situation but without filling in the details of the content, you invite your client to join you on a journey of discovery in his imaginary world.

Alternative 2

Coach: Imagine for a moment that I'm a fly. On the very day you just mentioned, I fly through the window into your room and sit on the wall, where I have a good view of everyone in the room. You and all your friends seem to be in the very best of spirits as you discuss all the great things that have happened in the last week. And there I am as a fly, listening in. What can I hear that you're talking about? What's making you all so cheerful? What will I be seeing?

Practicing this technique will make it increasingly easier to invite young clients to imagine their preferred future in detail. By describing what they want, instead of what they don't want, the emphasis is placed on what the future possibly might look like. A positive picture of a vivid and detailed preferred future becomes a picture that can be drawn into reality more easily. This new image of the preferred future is being projected as a full screen movie in 3D Technicolor with *Dolby surround sound* onto the inner home theater, one's own infinite imagination. Viewed together with the coach as if it were already taking place here and now, it becomes a possibility to consider as a future reality.

Changing perspective

Another possibility to help your clients describe their preferred future more easily is to use the perspective of an outsider, someone who perceives what happens in the future of the client in question.

Coach: If things go better for you in the future, what changes will your best friends notice? What will they say has changed for you?

To help create a complete and detailed picture, the following question is perhaps the most useful: "And what else?"

Coach: How will your best friends see that something has changed for you in the next year?
Client: They would see me joining classes more.
Coach: That sounds good. Can you think of anything else?
Client: I think they would also notice that I would make more of an effort and no longer play truant.
Coach: Oh, so you would attend school more often, join the classes, and do your best more. Anything more?

In most cases this gentle though persistent questioning provides you with more detailed information. However, in some situations, this will not help enough. Sometimes a client simply doesn't see the point of looking at a situation from an imaginary perspective. In that case, it is advisable for you to simply explain this. You then indicate that it may seem strange at first to have a conversation in this way but that it can certainly be useful to explore different directions of thinking, even when at first glance they seem unlikely to come into reality. Discussing the possible benefits of such a venture can often help your client to accept this more easily.

First things first

Sometimes your young client's thinking can be completely preoccupied by a problem that he's very concerned about and that he would rather discuss instead of focusing on the future. In such a situation, talking about his wishes for the future seems farfetched and irrelevant. It is then better to postpone a conversation about the future and to meet him where he is in that particular moment. It is very important for everyone, and young people are no exception, to feel that they are being heard and understood, far more important than talking about a preferred future and starting on a project involving change. Feelings and emotions need their space and must be sufficiently validated.

Experiment

This little exercise or experiment requires a pen, paper, an envelope, and approximately half an hour of your time. You can do this experiment with your client, but you can also benefit from doing it yourself. (Although you may be more accustomed to using a computer, this exercise is even more powerful when you write the letter by hand.)

Travel in your imagination into the future. Set a specific date, one, two, or even more years from now. You've just received a letter from a good friend whom you've not seen for several years and who lives on the other side of the world. You want to write a reply letter to this friend and tell him how you are and what you are doing these days. Start off your letter by writing the (future) date and "Dear ..." and go on to describe to your friend how you're enjoying the time of your life at that point in the future – as if it were *now*. Let your imagination run free without letting yourself be bothered by limiting thoughts. When you've finished writing, place the letter in the envelope, seal it, and put it somewhere safe to be opened at a later date. Maybe you even make a note in your diary of the date so that you can open the envelope and read what you've just written – in the future! You might be very surprised at what you read and the extent to which your life indeed resembles what you wrote.

Translating a fantasized future into workable goals

In case your client now *is* ready to think about his future and you have developed a clear picture together of what his future can look like – a future in which the initial problem no longer exists – it's time to move on and to use this information as a springboard for finding specific goals. These specific goals enable the client to bring his dream closer to reality, of course, all in small, feasible steps.

Distinguishing and choosing goals

Although it can be pleasant and tempting to continue talking with your client about some fantasy future, it may be clear that this would make little sense. Even teenagers and adolescents understand that in the end, some effort is expected of them to make this fantasy future, to some degree, come true. Their action is needed, new skills must be learned, or old ones need improvement. 'Something' or someone will have to change, or a simple continuation and perseverance on a previously mapped out and chosen path that is already proving to be successful is needed.

SMART

To help your client find out what that 'something' is and which skills he needs to learn or improve upon, you as the coach can help him to get clarity by first explaining to him a useful principle. The name of this management principle is the acronym *SMART*, in which goals are described as *Specific, Measurable, Acceptable, Realistic,* and *Time-related.*

The description of a dreamed future rarely meets these standards. It is merely a picture of an ideal, a beautiful wishful idea. To be able to work toward this perfect pictured future, you and the client first need to distinguish a specific goal that brings this future closer. Such a goal is much more limited than the dream image. It is more concrete, more tangible. It must be something that your young client specifically can do. It must be feasible. The *SMART* tool can be used to make the actual goal more specific and concrete. The client is then able to comprehend what exactly is expected of him to work on and what he can realistically achieve in the agreed time period. Perhaps it is unnecessary to mention here, but it is of course not the intention to use this *SMART* tool as an assessment. Such an application of the tool doesn't fit into a Solution Focused approach.

Here are some questions you can use to help your client find useful answers with the SMART tool:

- *Specific*: What exactly are you going to do? How would that look?
- *Measurable*: "What are visible changes that everybody will notice when you've reached your goal? What exactly will be different?

- *Acceptable*: Who benefits if you reach your goal? And how will these advantages weigh against any disadvantages?
- *Realistic*: What resources (talents, skills and competences, and previous experience) do you have that make you and others believe you truly can reach this goal?
- *Time-related*: What time frame have you set to reach your goal? When do you plan to celebrate your successful achievement? When can we plan the party?

Many readers will already have noticed that such a line of questioning is in itself already a mini-Mission Possible-program.

In addition, a goal must be interesting enough. Like everyone else, young people prefer to be challenged. They like to work on goals they have set themselves and that have not been imposed upon them by others. They must be able to own their choice and see the value. Only then will work motivation be optimal.

More than one goal

In order to make the dream of a future without problems come true, it's generally necessary to identify more than just a single goal; more than just one change will be required. Of course, in case it really is only about a single change, then the project is very straightforward – and it is clear which goal is the focus of the Mission Possible-program that you can start right away. But when there are more distinct goals, it's important to first make a list of all these goals. A conscious choice can then be made to decide which goal the client wants to work on first. It's fairly common for a client to experience some difficulty in choosing his first goal. Here you can provide valuable support. When it comes to choosing the goal that gets priority, there's a golden rule that applies, hidden in this question:

> "Of all these goals, which one will be the most effective in helping you make your dream come true?"

Or, put another way: "Which goal is going to help bring the dream closest fastest?" The client's answers to these questions should then make it easier to select the goal that is to be focused on.

Make it easy to look at goals

Experience shows that many clients are immediately able to select a goal that they would very much like to work toward. Simply going through this list of separate, identifiable goals helps to identify what's needed most. If the client were working through a list of *problems* instead of *goals*, then he would most certainly have a much harder time!

Tools for the toolbox

Key question

> "To bring your dream closer to becoming a reality, what do you need to be able to do, and what do you think you still need to learn?"

Together, coach and client make a long, and as detailed as possible, list of all the distinct skills, competences, and actions that contribute to realizing the preferred goal. Asking "What else can you think of?" is a great way of extending the list.

When no more answers are forthcoming, and the list is complete, it's time to start examining more closely. Relevant questions now include:

- "Of everything that's on your list, what's already in progress?"
- "Which of these skills do you already have or could you use in certain situations?"
- "What characteristics do you already have?"
- "In which situations have these already been effective for you?"

Such questions are an effective way of turning the list into a positive, supportive tool that makes the client aware of what he is capable of and what skills he already possesses that bring him closer to his goal. In this way, the *goal* appears more attainable and the *dream* becomes more realistic.

In that case, a lot of time would be wasted just finding out which problem was the root cause of all the other problems. Besides, when looking for the problem that underlies all other problems, a discussion could arise with other people involved (e.g., teacher, parents) who would probably have different opinions. Hmm, that would really be complicating.

A case study from practice

The following example comes from the practice of and was made available by Ben Furman:

Imagine for a moment that you are a teacher with a particularly troublesome group of students. You make a list of all the problems you're having with this class, and your list looks something like this:

1   The girls bully each other a lot.
2   The boys keep interrupting the lessons by misbehaving.

3   The parents of this group of students seem rather uninterested in the school achievements of their children.
4   Many of the students don't have the right books and study material because their parents experience financial problems.

This list looks rather heavy and oppressive. The presented problems seem so big that any teacher would lose motivation just by seeing this list of problems. Where in heaven's name should you start? You might try to see links between the various problems on your list. Perhaps you would try to analyze which problems were the root cause of all the other problems. It's quite a challenge, that's certain!

But imagine making the list again in a different way. Now it's not a list of class *problems* but of *common goals* that can be achieved. Your list now looks like this:

1   The girls are going to learn to be more tolerant of each other in the class so that everyone feels safer and more appreciated.
2   The boys are going to learn to quiet down and to behave during lessons.
3   Together, teacher and students are going to invent ways of involving their parents more closely with their schoolwork.
4   The school is going to find a way of ensuring that all the students have the right books and materials available.

The result is a short list of four specific goals. All four are important, to the extent that the question "Which of the four is the most important?" is no longer of interest. Instead, it's more realistic simply to look at which goal to tackle first, which raises this question: "Which of these goals is the most effective and is most likely to influence the other goals the most?"

A case study from practice: Michael

Michael has just turned 18. He has a serious disagreement with his adoptive parents about drinking alcohol and his daily use of soft drugs. Michael's parents are, to say the least, unhappy about his everyday use of both. According to them, it's the cause of all his problems at school and at home. Apparently, he is quite inconsiderate of others and regularly causes problems at home. He doesn't keep to his agreements, he soils his room without cleaning up – in fact he makes a mess everywhere he goes – and he lies in bed for days on end just watching online movies or playing computer games.

A behavioral therapist diagnosed Michael as suffering from an attachment disorder. His parents doubt the accuracy of this diagnosis because, in their opinion, Michael's antisocial behavior only began when he started drinking, smoking pot, and eating hallucinogenic mushrooms.

There's a long list of complaints about Michael from both the parents and the school, and he has also had a run-in with the law. A long series of interventions by various professionals and official agencies has not served to resolve any of these problems. Above all, because of the differences of opinion about the cause of Michael's problems, there is still no clarity about possible longer-term solutions.

However, when both Michael and his parents are asked to describe their preferred future, a future where the problems with Michael no longer exist, it is soon clear that there are many similarities. Both parties agree that Michael should leave home and find a place where he can be more independent. Together, they compile a list of everything that would be necessary in order to make this a reality. This list forms the basis for identifying goals. Even Michael understands that he's going to have to make an effort and expresses his willingness to cooperate. Because of this way of working, it becomes clear to Michael that he and his parents still have some common ground. As a result, he finds new motivation to communicate better and cooperate more. This is most certainly a better perspective for any problem solving.

When it happens that two or more significant goals of similar importance can be distinguished, the next step simply involves choosing which of the two will be given priority. Asking your client "Which goal would you prefer to work on first?" increases his motivation to complete the task. Generally speaking, young clients only have to glance briefly at their list in order to choose their first goal. That choice doesn't need to be justified. It suffices that it's the 'most attractive' choice at that moment. As one of my young clients once put it very clearly: "Sometimes I want a piece of chocolate and sometimes I'm more into having popcorn or potato chips." Imagine, though, that your client indeed experiences some difficulty choosing between the various possible goals. Then, asking your client the 'right' question can provide a redeeming answer: "Which of these goals would help you most to bring your preferred future closer?"

Turn negatives into positives

As mentioned before, the preferred future is all too often perceived from a negative point of view. Something should stop happening or should simply disappear! But simply 'stopping' something is almost always more challenging than starting something new. Think about 'stopping smoking' or 'stopping eating sweets'. It's definitely harder to be enthusiastic, proud, and motivated about achievements while at the same time trying to let go of an annoying habit or troublesome problem.

One thing is clear: what gets attention seems only to become bigger and more important. Trying to 'stop smoking' means that the focus is still on smoking instead of creating a healthier lifestyle. 'Stop telling lies' focuses on lying rather than on telling the truth. Take this well-known example of how this works linguistically: "For the next 10 seconds, you are *NOT* supposed to think about *pink* elephants." And guess what happens? Your imagination is filled with ... pink elephants!

Reframing

Luckily, most such negative instructions or goals can be reworded positively. In Michael's case, 'stop drinking alcohol' translates into 'stay sober' and 'stop abusing drugs' into 'stay clean'. 'Not playing truant' easily translates into 'attending classes'; 'stop biting your nails' translates into 'letting your nails grow'. It's simply a matter of looking for the right words to achieve the positively described result. It's important to note that the translated result may sometimes be different than simply the direct *opposite* of the problem. If the client stops playing truant, what will he then do alternatively? If he stops lying, maybe he'll either tell the truth instead or simply say nothing. If he wants to stop having arguments with his parents, maybe he'll try to live in peace with them, communicate better with them, or – more simply – just get along comfortably with them. It *can* be as easy as that. Just stopping with something – a negative goal – is not much fun; it's emotionally charged. But learning something new can be exciting and carries with it the hope of new opportunities and possibilities. Just think about the time you got your first guitar lesson or driving lesson and the new possibilities that opened up for you.

'Peeling' the goal

In Ben Furman's book on Kids'Skills, he describes how to peel a problem: splitting a complex problem into smaller, more doable ones. A great deal of discussion has taken place on this subject during the establishment of the Mission Possible-program with the clients and students I worked with to test the program on a trial-and-error basis. In practice, it appears to be quite confusing for many users to split up a problem. It brings them unintentionally into the trap of thinking and talking again from a problem focus. Peeling goals, splitting bigger ones into smaller subgoals, seems then much more obvious. In the past 10 years, this has proved to be an important tool in my practice as well as in training students who want to help their clients make the right choice of goal. In fact, this way of working prevents many pitfalls, such as working on too-large and therefore unrealistic goals or working on a goal the client feels no ownership of.

Trial-and error

I have developed this protocol as a tool for correctly finding a goal for the Mission Possible-program in order to give more guidance to coaches who want to ensure a successful trajectory with their clients. Moreover, it has turned out to be a useful instrument that easily blends into other work forms, as a result of which you as a coach have more options based on your client's choice and preferences. The peel protocol lets itself easily intertwine with other usable, Solution Focused work forms such as the 'circle technique' (see Tools for the toolbox page 58), 'mind-mapping', and 'drawing your conversation'. Here, I will first explain the five-question peel protocol as I've developed and researched it. The explanation of the circle technique you can find in the Tools for the toolbox.

Advantages of using the peel protocol

There are many good reasons for using this step-by-step protocol to determine the actual goal your client will work on. Of course, an experienced coach in the Solution Focused approach and its typical accompanying language will most certainly be able to do without it. But since there's more than one way leading to Rome, in practice, it appears to work well for many who are less experienced. After all, not everyone is already an expert in quickly producing the most effective open questions. It requires a lot of training and experience. And although the Solution Focused and progress-focused approach may seem simple at first glance, using these approaches can have many pitfalls. That's why it can be helpful to have a well-defined structure of questions, which will always ensure a successful outcome. And even within this standardized outline of questioning, the protocol leaves you plenty of room for flexibility and creativity. Within this structure, you will be able to vary, as long as you learn where you can allow yourself some room for improvisation. Within this protocol, which is meant to help you stay out of trouble, there are a number of fixed questions. Language simply isn't neutral: just changing the words of a question a little can produce a different effect and therefore evoke a different answer. Strictly following the five questions from the peel protocol will ensure that they provide you with the desired effect.

A list of advantages:

- There is immediately interactive collaboration between you and your client;
- You always place the initiative with the client;
- Together you conduct a detailed investigation into the desired situation and what it takes to achieve it;
- During this research, all subskills and subgoals are distinguished, including the very basic (read: obvious) and easily accessible;

- The resources step (step 6) can be fully integrated in this first Mission Possible step. This step has therefore become a natural part of the process;
- All existing and usable skills, talents, traits, experiences, and other useful resources are immediately covered here;
- The client receives a constant overview of what he can do and what therefore needs no change. As a result, the goal seems to come a lot closer;
- The client has a better self-confidence and motivation platform right at the start of the Mission Possible process;
- The choice for a specific goal to work on becomes easier;
- The client himself chooses which goal can bring the desired situation closer. This guarantees ownership immediately;
- Working together on the peel protocol gives energy and a lot of reason for optimism.

How to overcome a possible disadvantage

A single downside to the way the peel protocol works – honesty commands me to mention that here too – is its rather linguistic approach. Of course, it may happen that a client with whom you are working appears to have less-than-average language skills available. In such a case, even writing on a flip chart can be a difficult hurdle to overcome. Then, of course, it's completely okay that you ask for his permission to write it down for him.

Solutions to overcome language barriers

To help him find answers to the somewhat challenging questions of the protocol, it might make a huge difference to abstain from talking all together and engage in a mutual roleplay. Just by pretending for a moment, your client can present everything he wants to share with more ease, while you say out loud all that you see him do. You can then offer your client the choice to write on the flip chart or not. Using a magnetic board with pictograms, drawing your own pictograms, or even tearing pictures from magazines and making a 'mood board' can also offer solutions here. You as a coach must dare to let yourself be surprised and fully utilize the qualities of the young client. I often notice that young people are fantastic as cartoon artists, quickly and with humor able to draw what they want to express. And some of them find it super fun to be a director of their own roleplay movie.

Preparation

Earlier in this chapter about step 1, you read how you are able to ensure that you and your client together translate an existing problem into a preferred situation: You ask the question about the desired situation. To ideally facilitate this question, it is nice to have a large sheet of paper and markers ready for writing and drawing. I myself prefer to do this entire step 1 process together with my client, standing in front of a flipchart. When both you and your client take a marker in your hands, you can equally participate in a truly co-creative process.

The peel protocol in five clear steps

Answer the following questions together and follow the instructions faithfully. Remember that only one question is needed per step of the protocol, even though there are more potentially useful questions written here.

Question 1: The question about the desired situation

Ask one of the following questions and write the answer together on the flip chart: "What do you want instead of your problem? What is your preferred situation? What does your future look like when your problem no longer exists? Imagine that ..." Here you have several options.

Let your client choose one of the answers to explore further through this protocol and ask him to write it down at the top of a blank sheet of paper:

Question 2: The question from a different perspective about the details of the desired situation

"What is someone who has achieved [now state the desired situation] able to do or learn? What skill or skills does he apply to achieve this desired situation? What does someone do who [state the desired situation]?" or "What do you do when you apply this skill?" "What does anyone need to be able to learn, do, or achieve?"

Here you also have different options for the same question. Choose whichever question works best in your client's situation.

Making lists to structure the process

In this process of answering the above question, now create as long a list as possible of (sub-)skills, characteristics, and talents that are necessary to achieve the above preferred goal. Especially remember to think of very obvious things, too. For example: for concentrating in class, it is at least nice if someone knows which table he should sit at, how he can gently sit down, take out his books and place them open and on the right page in front of him, and so on. The list can be super long, preferably containing somewhere between 8 and 15 different things. And of course, you are allowed to help your client create that list. "I know a good one too! Can I write it down?"

If your client comes to a halt during the conversation, you can actively further the process by thinking and writing along. Anything you contribute that helps to co-create a list as long as possible and to distinguish as many subskills and sub goals as is remotely possible is very welcome. And because this part of the process takes place right at the start of your contact with your young client, such a dynamic and positively oriented collaboration also helps to promote confidence in the collaboration itself.

Question 3: The question about what's already there, previous successes

"Which of the things on this list can you do or are you already doing well?" Ask the young person to put a smiley on every item on the list that is going well. Asking further at some points, to see how that goes, may be a reason for the young person to experience success even before you are well on your way with Mission Possible. There is often much more than you think, and this is the right time to recognize and appreciate it together. A growing sense of competence in the young person thus supports the growth of motivation.

Question 4: A variation on the question about exceptions to the problem

"And which of the remaining things on the list can you already do a little? When or where will they succeed? And what is different in that situation, as a result of which it already succeeds?"

Ask the young person to put a half (vertically cut) smiley for these points. A half smiley can easily be made into a whole one later.

Question 5: The last question of the protocol is the question of the preference of the young person himself

"Which thing (or which things) still remains on the list? Which of these things would help you most to reach your chosen goal? Which thing would help you achieve your goal best?"

Systemic 'side effects'

Purposely let your client make a choice entirely for what he prefers to work on, even if that choice isn't immediately the most obvious or supported by the environment. Such an autonomous decision is always better than one that is imposed. For you, it is appropriate here to respect your young client's choice and to trust that working toward his goal will also bring his other goals closer. Finally, through working on this one goal, from a systemic point of view, usually other partial goals also change. One 'drop in the ocean' has a big ripple effect.

Onward to Mission Possible step 2: the benefits

After this question protocol, in which you and your client have 'dissected' the desired situation to the bone and you have mapped out what no longer needs to be addressed, your client is ready to move on to step 2: the benefits of reaching the goal. But it all too often happens that this step looking at the possible benefits has already been extensively discussed during the making of the above list. Talking about achievable goals in a reachable near future, as well as talking about past successes, simply makes hungry for more. Remember that the chosen goal must be small enough to be achievable but challenging enough to make the client feel he has to work for it. Small, achievable, *and* at least some effort-demanding steps enhance the chance of success and growing self-confidence. Moreover, they are achieved much faster than 'giant leaps'. Thus, the value of the goal lies not only in the intended benefits that can work as a reward but also in working on the goal itself.

Step 2: The benefits

When your client is facing a problem that he really wants to solve, there's clearly a solid foundation for working toward that solution: he already shows that he is *willing* to work and cooperate. The next step is to formulate the goal that will help resolve his issue; if *this* step is successful, then he is well on his way to completing the task.

When he also realizes that he himself needs to take action, then he's definitely ready to be considered as a client and equally ready to start.

But all too often this is precisely the moment when doubts start occurring:

> "Do I *really* want to do this? Is this the only solution? Is this my only goal right now? What's the best thing to do? What should I choose? And how can I choose when I have no way of knowing what the consequences of my choice will be?"

Although these are all perfectly normal questions, unfortunately, they tend to weaken the motivation for change that's just before slowly, hesitantly being awakened. The best and most logical way forward at this point is to take a close look at and identify all possible benefits of proceeding toward the goal.

Antidote against insecurity

Thoroughly summarizing all possible benefits is a great way to inject new life into the client's motivation and, at the same time, remove any doubts and insecurity that may be present in the beginning.

Such a summary has a further advantage: the goal will most likely become clearer, perhaps even better defined. In this process, too, the client may redefine or at least slightly reformulate his goal, possibly proving the existence of even more benefits.

Motivation

In order to set goals, it's first necessary to have a clear picture of what the future should look like. Setting goals *and* achieving them successfully is already quite a difficult task for most adults. It's not much different for teenagers and adolescents, who are busy discovering all the possibilities open to them and are faced with having to choose their direction to follow. In fact, their options are so diverse and comprehensive that it is already difficult enough to gain a clear perspective – let alone to make a sensible decision with any ease. A lack of overview and experience with the consequences of all these options can lead to feeling overwhelmed, which can feel quite paralyzing. In such conditions, then, 'not choosing' seems a better option.

The hardest choice of all

However, it turns out that in the end, it's much harder to motivate yourself for *not* having made a choice. This generally results in a sense of emptiness, boredom, and lack of energy. From such a state of mind, it's extremely complicated to find a positive outlook on the future. However, a positive future perspective is an important precondition for anyone who wants to have a sense of well-being. In the absence of a positive expectation for the future, happiness remains an unattainable ideal.

For someone already feeling unhappy, it's an enormous challenge to work up sufficient motivation to pursue a far-off goal somewhere in the future. A number of factors are required in order to get optimally motivated for such a goal.

The previous chapter, 'What is the Mission Possible-program?' describes how these factors can be split up into the *five themes* that comprise the steps of the Mission Possible-program. I choose to repeat them here once more, since they are crucial for fully understanding the steps, as well as a basis for optimal, autonomous motivation.

The five psychological factors that enhance motivation[1]

1   *Choosing the goal and owning that choice*

A primary condition that must be satisfied is that the client can identify with the selected goal. Even if it's primarily a goal that's been suggested (or even imposed) by someone else, he must be totally clear that it is also *his* choice and that it's sufficiently important, interesting, and attractive for him (an internalized extrinsic goal). For appropriate questions to achieve this ownership of the goal, see the previous discussion on Step 1: the peel protocol.

2   *Seeing the value of the goal*

Subsequently, here it's intentional to look at *why* this goal is interesting and important to the client. Questions that are now appropriate include:

"What is it about this goal that makes it worthwhile for you?"
"What distinct benefits do you see about reaching this goal?"
"What good will it do you in the end?"

3   *Having the confidence that the goal can be achieved*

Here you have to help your client to look at all that can strengthen his self-confidence and good faith in a positive outcome. This is a perfect moment to become aware of all existing resources. After all, once the client is *aware* of them, he can put them to good use. Key questions here include:

"What makes you and also others believe that this is a feasible goal for you?"
"What skills, talents, abilities, and experiences do you already have that will help you to achieve this goal?"
"What makes you think you can achieve this specific goal?"
"And what previous experiences make you confident that you will be successful this time too?"

4   *Experiencing progress*

When the client clearly observes progress in the desired direction and is able to appreciate it, his trust in his own abilities is growing along with his self-confidence, creating a more positive self-image. All such experiences of moving forward, even when this progress is achieved with micro-successes, nourish the client's desire for more. Experiences of progress are perfect accelerators for motivation.

5   *Being willing to accept and deal with possible failure and setbacks*

It's normal to experience failure. There's no reason for failure to affect positive developments in both the Mission Possible-program and a growing self-confidence. But it *is* important to include when making plans and to be prepared to deal with it.

Distinguishing possible benefits

The five most important preconditions for optimizing motivation make this very clear: one of the crucial factors is the conviction that the goal is sufficiently *interesting and attractive* to pursue. This implies, in essence, that the client must be clear about the benefits of realizing his intended goal – benefits for both himself and the significant people in his life.

Obviously, the client will choose a goal that produces benefits; otherwise, there's no point in it being on his list of possible goals. It is nevertheless true that the client may not at this stage be aware of the range of advantages accruing to the attained goal. What better way to explore all possible details than to take a step beyond just thinking about them and to discuss them with someone else? There's a golden rule that applies here: the longer the list of distinct benefits, the higher the level of motivation for achieving the goal. Put another way: the longer the list, the more desirable the goal is.

The Mission Possible workbook pays considerable attention to this step and, because of the simple, clear questions, requires little in the way of additional explanation.

You can invite your client to pay extra attention to this step and to review it with regularity, serving to enlarge the desirability of the goal and increase his motivation. For the client, it's very pleasant to discover more benefits as the program progresses, all of which in turn fuel his willingness to persist.

Note

1 Based on and adapted from principles expressed by Tapani Ahola and Ben Furman in their books on Reteaming and Creating Solution Focused Working Environments

Chapter 4

Building trust and self-confidence

Two key factors for motivation are at the heart of the first two themes, summed up in the phrases 'it's *my* goal' and 'this goal has value for me'. These two themes coincide with the first two steps of the Mission Possible-program: step 1: Goal and step 2: Benefits. These two steps are the first layer of the foundation for the Mission Possible process.

The Mission Possible steps 3, 4, and 7, belonging to the third theme, are focused on strengthening the client's confidence in his abilities and potential. To this end, all possible different sources and resources are called upon, using as many internal and external resources as possible. Here, you help your client to become consciously aware of every source and resource that is already present. And as you move into the next Mission Possible steps, you are gradually adding new ones.

In step 3, Support, significant people from your client's environment are invited to actively provide support. And apart from the most important encouragement from these supporting people, your client can choose a symbol in step 4, Symbol, to help him improve his self-confidence even more. After all, even the very best of supporters is not going to be available 24/7. Therefore, choosing a symbol for personal encouragement is a step that a client takes independently, requiring no help or actual presence from anyone else.

In step 7, Scaling, you can help your client gain more insight in his process by integrating all previous steps in this one exercise. In this way, your client's motivational platform becomes firmly anchored. After all, once insights have come into awareness, they have become practically applicable and repeatable resources for future situations.

Step 3: Support

While working on goals that are still projected in the future, young people experience all sorts of challenges. It can be a lonely process for a client, in which he finds himself sometimes faced with difficult emotions. Admitting that he isn't able to do something yet or that he still has to learn something also confronts him with feelings of incompetence and powerlessness. And those particular feelings are usually difficult to share with others, since they are often triggers for even more difficult feelings: shame and guilt. Being involved in such a delicate process, it is more than just nice for your client if he's not alone. It is of the utmost importance and in the case of this Mission Possible even a necessary part of the program! A solid support system must be created to help him carry out the difficult task of successfully achieving the goal he has set. Recognizing and accepting the challenges of this difficult task gives space for a realistic view on both expectations and results. It is designed to make it easier for the client to accept help. Well-known adages like 'No man is an island' and 'Two heads are better than one' are definitely appropriate when building a support system!

The value of having supporters

In their pursuit of individuality and their development toward adulthood and independence, adolescents have a tendency to adopt an 'I can manage on my own' attitude.

This attitude, this drive toward independence, is strengthened by a sense of loneliness that an adolescent can experience, for shorter or longer periods, during this stage of his life. "Apparently I have to do it all on my own" seems to be the underlying and *limiting* conviction. Such a contracted state of mind generally makes it harder to trust others or ask for help, let alone accept it. This attitude, unfortunately, often results in an increasing state of isolation while he struggles to deal with his problems.

Healing social environment

Mission Possible is designed to avoid these negative aspects by inviting the client to take steps that will create a robust system to support his process. The intention is to create a solid support system that serves him when the going gets tough and that provides ongoing encouragement during the entire program.

And, in addition, Mission Possible aims to embed the client in a supportive social structure to ensure a process of resocialization. The program's support structure is an excellent means of helping your client explore and develop his social skills, as well as healing once-damaged relationships.

Who qualifies as a supporter?

Everything and everyone that is able to provide support and encouragement during your client's Mission Possible-program qualifies as a potential 'supporter'. In the first place, he will probably consider family, friends, teachers, coaches and other significant people in his life. But the remarkable thing is that a pet, nature, and even deceased loved ones or pets can play an important role as supporters.

Working toward a goal is, in most cases, more than just an individual effort. It's very rare that clients manage completely without any help from others. Everyone, at some time, needs validation, encouraging support, and appreciation from other people. Some need less than others, but the need for positive relationships and connection is fundamental for and present in all human beings. Using this inherent and basic need as a powerful resource in the Mission Possible program the young client is invited to reach out and find support for and confirmation of his growing self-confidence.

Being clear and specific in asking for help

Perhaps this sounds easy, but it's not a process that happens automatically. In order to get as many people as possible willing to be his supporter and to make the best use of their contributions, the client must take a number of specific steps.

First of all, he needs to consider who would be supportive to his process and how each supporter specifically can contribute to his support. Supporters must therefore be very clearly informed of what is expected of them. In the absence of this first step, a supporter can even have a negative influence on the process and the client's motivation, ultimately leading to failure. The importance of this step must therefore certainly not be underestimated. Think, for example, of having a supporter without any previous consideration of or agreement on how he or she is going to give support. In such a case, support might be easily promised but fall short when needed most.

A case study from practice: Jeffrey

Jeffrey is a 13-year-old boy who, after seeing the school doctor, is referred to my practice. He's an eighth grader in primary school and is soon to start his first year in high school. The doctor expressed her concerns regarding Jeffrey being obese. She suggested Jeffrey talk to me about his options to do something about the problem and so save him from potential health risks.

After a few minutes into the conversation, it becomes clear that Jeffrey is not at all happy about his weight either and that he is extremely anxious to see this change. He even says he has already tried a few times. On both occasions, he successfully lost some weight but put it on again after a while when leaving his dietary regime.

Coach: What helped you to be successful in losing weight those two times, Jeff?

Jeffrey: I made a plan for the whole week in advance and helped my mom do the grocery shopping. I could then pick the food I liked and that was also fitting well in my diet, like lots of fresh veggies and lean meat.

Coach: Ah, so you were really involved in the preparation of your food, shopping together with your mom. That's great. In what other ways did your mom support your diet plans?

Jeffrey: Uhm, well, she didn't really support it, I guess.

Coach: What do you mean? I assumed since you shopped for groceries together that she was indeed supporting you.

Jeffrey: Well. Yes, maybe at first. But then, after a while, she didn't want me to join her while shopping anymore, and we kind of stopped. And then eventually, it became too hard to stick to eating healthy. Then I started eating along with everybody else again and regained the weight.

Coach: I see. I'm sorry to hear this, Jeffrey. It seems to me you really tried your best. What do you think needs to be different if you would try again?

Jeffrey: I think someone needs to talk to my mom first. She needs help understanding a few things.

Coach: Right. What things does she need to understand, Jeffrey?

Jeffrey: Well, things like how it is for me. How it feels when classmates make fun of me and how they don't want to be associated with me. And also, I want her to know that I *do* understand that my diet food is more expensive and that I don't take that for granted. Maybe there are alternatives, cheaper options that also fit into my diet. I mean, she worried, and she felt it was too hard to keep up with.

Coach: Yes, I think you're spot-on right, Jeff. You need more and better support, and also your mom needs some support. It's a big goal, but it can be done, and certainly when you are so well motivated and understand already so much about what it takes. You have proven that you *can* do it. What kind of support would you like to have next time? And who else do you think would make you and your mom a good supporter?

Jeffrey: I think I need at least a few more. It would take a supporter who knows about health food, and maybe also one who knows about balancing budgets and cheaper alternatives. And I personally would like to have a supporter to talk to about myself and being obese, and all that. And of course, I might also need a supporter that can provide or at least join in on some healthy activities, like sporting together. I like swimming a lot, but it's not fun just being on my own.

Coach: Wow! What fantastic ideas you already have for more effective support, Jeffrey. Yes, let's look at our options.

Need for diversity

And *second*, since not all supporters are equal in their abilities and possibilities, it's important for the client to create as large a support group as possible. Obviously, the more diverse the group of supporters is, the more external resources the client has at his disposal during his Mission Possible process.

A diversity of ages and life experience as well can provide enormous enrichment. By helping your client collect as many as possible different supporters, less obvious choices become visible, opening up new possibilities that can be explored and exploited.

Just like in sports

The supporter's tasks are wide-ranging and include moral and practical support, encouragement, validation, appreciation for the client's efforts as well as his successes, observation of progress and success, willingness to brainstorm about useful suggestions and ideas, healing relationships, and repairing a damaged reputation. Obviously, there's a lot to gain with having supporters.

In the world of sports, it's perfectly normal to have supporters. Can you imagine a football club without its crowd of supporters to watch the game and celebrate its success? People to train and coach, people to cheer them on, to manage the club, to take care of finances, mow the field, clean the locker rooms, and maintain the materials are all equally needed. And all enjoy being a part of it. Without each and any one of them, the quality of the game would be less. Well, supportership in the Mission Possible-program works exactly the same way. If organized well, it's an interactive and mutually nourishing experience. The client feels supported and encouraged, which helps him achieve more. The supporter enjoys the client's success as well as the part he plays in his friend's or family member's achievements. By contributing actively to the client's success, the supporter feels appreciated and knows that he is doing something worthwhile. This way, the client–supporter relationship can be a true example of a *win-win* interaction.

Handle with care

You, as the coach, have an important task in facilitating the largest and most varied 'supporters club' as possible in cooperation with your client. With good reason, you need to invest the necessary time and attention here to ensure the effectiveness of this step, even in case – and sometimes this happens – your client at the start of the process indicates that he can't see any point in recruiting supporters. It's quite common that the suggestion of inviting supporters brings up feelings of shame or shattered pride that can come along with admitting to having a problem. Much more important than to force a client into taking this step is to respect those feelings and tread carefully. It's much better to wait until there's an opportunity further along in the process to raise this point again and maybe even to wait for the first successes to occur.

It's equally common to address this step yet again at other moments during the process; that's part of the flexibility inherent to the 'nonchronological' but tailor-made 'coaching from one step behind the shoulder' approach of the Mission Possible-program.

Midterm reviews

Equally valuable are the interim evaluations during the process. It's always good to keep a close eye on the value of the supporters and regularly check how they are positively contributing to your client's process. Is an initially chosen supporter still effective later on in the process? Do the supporters do what they have agreed to do in the beginning? How does your client experience their support? Should initial agreements with supporters perhaps be revised and adjusted along the way? Discussing support and how it is of value to help your client achieve his goal is an ongoing part of every session.

Relevant questions for such an interim supporter evaluation are these:

"How are you getting on with your supporters?"
"What did you do to keep in touch with them?"
"How useful are your supporters in your process? What sort of support do you receive from them?"
"How do you experience the support you're getting?"
"You made agreements with your supporters some time ago, when you started out; is it necessary to review those agreements and maybe make some changes? How could your supporters be even more helpful?"

Inviting supporters

In general, your client himself will indicate which people he feels suitable as his supporters. You, as his coach, can help him to further explore possible candidates and their specific role in the client's process. It's your task to ask questions from different points of view, and the Mission Possible Workbook provides supportive examples that can be applied. The questions help clarify who the client can best approach as well as how suitable they are as a supporter. In addition, ask your client specifically what contribution he would like to receive from each particular supporter.

Preferably the next step for your client is to invite the candidate supporter for a personal meeting, during which he is invited to contribute to the client's Mission Possible-program. Your client can expand the invitation by adding an indication of the kind of support he wants to receive from each supporter.

This meeting immediately creates a sense of cooperation in which client and supporter each play an equally important part in the process.

If your client has difficulty in asking supporters personally, a realistic option is to consider writing a letter, either by him or together with you. Of course, these days, it's perfectly acceptable to approach potential supporters through social media – e-mail, WhatsApp, or whatever platform is currently in vogue. An important reminder for your client is that his messages should only be visible for the individuals concerned and not accidently shared publicly.

To illustrate this step, read more about Josh and how he's getting on with his Mission Possible journey.

A case study from practice: Josh (this time without Marsha) continuation

Josh comes to a coaching meeting, and this time he's alone. The theme today is all about setting up a network of supporters. Although I broached the subject with him at an earlier meeting, he had been clear about it not being the right moment for him to start inviting supporters to help him. When I pursue the subject, Josh eventually admits that he feels rather embarrassed – letting potential supporters know that he has a problem feels to him like a weakness, some sort of disgrace.

In this meeting, I ask him if he could imagine a way of inviting supporters without ever mentioning his problem. Josh starts thinking about this. Then, all of a sudden, he starts laughing.

Josh: How silly of me! Of course I can. I simply tell them that I want to learn something new.
Coach: Right on, Josh! Top marks! OK, what next?

With a broad grin on his face he starts naming all the people he'd like to approach and ask to be his supporter. To my surprise and appreciation, he adds two interesting names to his increasingly long list: his sister Marsha and his deceased father. Josh explains that although he's always creating trouble for Marsha, she's nevertheless a wise choice.

Josh: She's really pretty smart!

As to his father, he's rather reticent at this moment: "It's difficult. But he really does feel like a supporter, I mean, when I think about him ..."

Coach: Do you think about him a lot?
Josh: Yes, I do.
Coach: What do you think your dad would say or do if you were to ask him right now if he'd be your supporter?
Josh: Oh, that's easy – he'd immediately say yes. And y'know what, he'd pat me on the shoulder, too. He always did that when we talked.
Coach: Well, Josh, can you imagine that he would do that now, I mean, pat you on the shoulder in this moment?
Josh: I don't even have to imagine – it just feels that way *now*.
Coach: That's impressive, Josh! You two still seem to have a very strong bond!

Josh nods, clearly deeply moved: "Y'know ... He's just the best supporter anyone could ever wish for. Always was, always will!"

Coach: Wow! So, your dad is still your best supporter. That's really terrific! And how could that work, I mean, be useful for you *now*, do you think? Can you explain to me?

Josh: Uhh ... well, I just have to think about him, and I know exactly what he would say. It's as if I can hear him talking to me in this moment. And y'know, sometimes I really feel that he's really here, too ...

Coach: How beautiful, Josh! I'm lost for words. Would you like to tell me more? Where do you feel his presence?

Josh: *[Indicates a point close to and behind his right shoulder]* About here.

Coach: How is that for you, to feel him so close by?

Josh: What exactly do you mean?

Coach: Can you describe what you feel in such a moment? How you know? I'm intrigued.

Josh: It feels ... warm, it feels like having a friend here, someone who's always here for me.

I relax and let the silence do its work. Josh, too, says nothing for a while. We both let the marvel of this profound awareness fully sink in. Josh is alone in his imagination, close to his father and this newly discovered possibility of having him close by as a supporter instead of far off as the dead father he continues to miss. For my part, as therapist, coach, and also simply as a human being, I relish the warmth of the deep sense of gratitude and wonder; gratitude for these unexpected gifts born of this contact and the richness of the experience for us both; wonder, too, for the innate intelligence of the heart that, once tapped, always finds its way to express itself authentically.

The role for the coach

The role that is reserved for you as the coach in the process of recruiting supporters can be a multifaceted one. It happens frequently that a client asks his coach to participate as one of his supporters. Of course, every coach is free to decide for himself what's best and whether to honor such a request. My personal experience is that the effort involved in being both coach *and* supporter is usually small, but with great effect. A client usually appreciates that his coach has certain professional restrictions concerning the extent to which his coach can spend extra time on him. But it's perfectly possible to negotiate ways in which you can perhaps give additional support and validation above and beyond the meetings involved in the Mission Possible-program.

How to support your client outside the session room

Apart from the (nowadays obvious) use of email – although the current laws on privacy and processing of personal data do require that this medium be used only with the necessary attention and secure safeguards – using online apps and chat apps are a less suitable medium for this. They might seem an easy and, to most young people, available way of exchanging contact, but hold security and privacy risks. Though many will consider it old-fashioned, it is my experience that a simple postcard, a phone call, a chance chat passing by each other in the hallway can work real wonders for your client when it comes to experiencing a sense of your support, as long as you make clear agreements.

How to give substance to your role

For many a client it will take time before he's built up his network, so the coach will, for a while – and certainly at the start of the program – be his main supporter. Recruiting supporters, winning back trust and repairing an all-too-often damaged reputation simply will take some time. In the intervening period, the coach can be a fantastic asset to the growing support system.

The attentive reader will have noticed that the facilitator – conveniently referred to as the coach in this book – has a task that is all but rigidly defined. The coach's most important task can best be described in the carefully chosen words: 'holding the space' (Steve de Shazer and Y. Dolan, 2007, *More than miracles; The state of the art of Solution Focused brief therapy*).

Being fully present

This expression of 'holding the space' describes your undivided and conscious presence in the moment. You become totally subservient to the process your client is involved in. And although this process mainly takes place within your client, it also takes place in the interaction between the two of you. At first glance, this expression may sound a little vague, but in fact it is not. Being present, observing, attuning, and connecting attentively in the moment are the required characteristics and skills for any Solution Focused conversation. Solutions present themselves almost automatically by your being fully present instead of thinking a few steps ahead; by attentively observing all usable signs – including the nonverbal ones – and making them immediately available; by moving flexibly with that which presents itself right here and now. Sometimes this 'flow' happens so wonderfully that it seems almost magical. But don't be fooled; it's just as pragmatic as it is magic: watch what happens, pick up what information presents itself in the moment, examine it curiously, and see how it can be used.

Or, much better said, invite your client to observe what presents itself in the moment, to examine it closely and curiously, and let him discover how it can be used in his favor! It really is as simple as that!

Step 4: Symbol

Ever since humans have lived on this planet, the world has been full of symbols and symbolism. They can be found everywhere, in every culture – from cave drawings from prehistoric times to the graffiti tags on concrete walls made by modern urban artists – and most people use them without ever stopping to think about it. Yet these symbols have enormous influence on how people think and behave. The contemporary world of marketing and advertising is a perfect example of where symbols are consciously and cleverly used to influence customers' purchasing patterns. Symbolism is a form of communication, one that goes far beyond just the visual aspect.

Positive influence

Consider for a moment the background music in shops, designed to put customers in the mood for buying … or the special spray used by inventive garages for the car interior after a regular service as a reminder of that 'new car' feeling … or the delicious smell of baking or of freshly brewed coffee to stimulate positive responses from potential buyers as they view the house that's for sale …

In these examples, symbolism is used somewhat manipulatively, intending to subconsciously influence people's behavior, but there is no shortage of possibilities for using symbols in a perfectly positive and supportive way. Symbols can be extremely useful as a resource in supporting the change processes that young people go through during their Mission Possible-program trajectories.

A helping hand

Most people surround themselves with many things that have a deeper significance for them, even when they aren't always consciously aware of it. Think for a moment about older people who have a special place for the many photos of their children, grandchildren, and even great-grandchildren. Or the young girl who is so charmed by a Walt Disney cartoon princess that she collects posters, photos, and other attributes as well, of course, as all the movies. Or, specifically regarding adolescents and young adults, witness the enormous rise in popularity of getting a tattoo.

It's very human to give meaning to symbols as a visual expression of emotional, psychological, and spiritual values. As such, symbols are part of daily life, and their function must definitely not be underestimated. For some, they're a mainstay. For others, they help give meaning to life. For yet others, symbols nourish a sense of being part of something greater and grander than just getting up in the morning and going to work every day. That's probably why so many people nowadays have a statue of Buddha in their house or garden, even though they are not religious or living as Buddhists. Symbols provide direction and guidance.

Symbols as an independent source of support

How do you, when using the Mission Possible-program with your client, make use of this very human trait? How can you make sure your client has all resources available at all times, even when supporters might not be? For that purpose of having independent support 24/7, symbols make great assets.

With this step, you ask your client to choose a symbol for the goal he's pursuing. You ask him to choose something or someone that represents his goal and makes it in some way visible and more tangible. The symbol performs the valuable task of bringing an initially abstract goal in the future closer to the here and now reality. The symbol supports the client, reinforcing his motivation, through his regular and direct contact with it.

A physical reminder

Young people are more than ever before accustomed to using pictures and expressing themselves through imagery: a simple online video clip contains the visual and auditory communication that is part of their daily life. Since it's an important and inherent part of the world they now occupy, it's an excellent reason for putting symbols to use as a resource in Mission Possible-programs.

At the right moment, it's up to the coach to ask questions like these:

> "What thing, person, photo, word, expression, tune, or whatever you can think of could be a symbol for you of the goal you want to achieve? Something that, when you see it, touch it, or think about it, will remind you of that goal ..."

What the client chooses is entirely up to him, as long as it's *his* symbol that represents *his* goal or the program as a whole. What has proven to be most effective is something that the client can keep with him the whole time, something that, for example, fits in his pocket or can be worn on his neck, wrist, clothes, or smartphone. Whatever it is, it serves to remind him at all times of the goal he's aiming at.

Symbols: signs of commitment

Of course, whatever your client chooses is all right, as long as the symbol he chooses is a positive and constant reminder of his goal. However, much more can be achieved with a symbol. The chosen object, in whatever form, can also symbolize the client's personal dedication in addition to the function of just being a physical reminder. In fact, it can also symbolize the choice of committing to change in itself. This is a more abstract approach to choosing a symbol, which refers less substantively to the chosen goal and therefore requires some insight from the client from a higher perspective. It can certainly be worthwhile to increase the value of the chosen symbol by inviting your client to think about it a little more deeply. If he answers the question with 'yes', then the door is wide open for a conversation that explores matters more deeply: "How could the symbol you choose also symbolize your decision and commitment to reach your goal?"

A case study from practice: Peter

Peter is seeing his therapist after dealing with a long period of feeling depressed. He's been working on conquering all kinds of fears for the past six months. These fears have gradually crept up on him in the past three years and made him retreat from society more and more, up to the point that he is no longer able to take care of himself in a healthy way. After being in a group therapy program for one year without experiencing much progress, Peter is now coming to my practice for a more tailor-made and Solution Focused approach. He wants to conquer his fear, starting with getting up in the morning and going out for a little walk in the streets. At this point in his therapy, Peter and I are discussing his choice of symbol: a picture of a beautiful swimming tiger.

Coach: So, you've chosen a symbol of a swimming tiger, Peter. And you've made a decision about how you're going to work toward your goal. Tell me, how, do you think, can this symbol of the swimming tiger represent your decision to work on your goal and the way you're committing to your process of overcoming your fears?

Peter: The swimming tiger stands not only for the fearless and powerful animal that walks his path alone. That, I feel, is me, but without fear. It also represents relaxation and feeling safe, and allowing myself to trust that things in the end will be all right. A tiger only swims when he feels perfectly alone and safe, because he's more vulnerable then.

Coach: That's a very interesting thought, Peter. And how does that apply to you and your Mission Possible process? Could you explain this a bit more to me?

Peter: Sure. I mean, that I find it difficult to trust people and situations sometimes. And although I do not mind being alone and doing the necessary work to reach my goal – I really *am* determined – I see I need to be less on my guard too. There's no such thing as achieving anything special if you're not willing to take risks. I see that I need to let go of this tension I feel all the time a little. Trust more, and risk more … that is, at least I need to be willing to let people nearer and not isolate myself all the time … open my curtains in the morning and let the sunlight in … It's what this swimming tiger is representing to me. The open space of the pool, surrounded by the deep forest, looks scary and inviting at the same time. And the tiger dares to take on the invitation of the open water, not knowing what is around him in the forest. I can tell he loves to swim. It's also about allowing myself to feel joy, I guess, like the tiger enjoys the water.

Coach: Peter, I have no doubts that you have chosen the right symbol for you and your process. If it has already brought on all of these profound insights in your own situation and how you want it to change, I can only feel deep respect and gratitude. It's amazing how well thought through you have taking this step. I'm sure this image of the swimming tiger will support you in many ways along the way.

Peter: Y'know, I've been thinking … Maybe I will have a tattoo of this picture when I am well on my way.

Coach: I'm not a tattoo-person myself, to be honest. I see many odd ones pass by and then always think what they'll look like in

> say … 20 or 30 years. But if I could see one good reason to
> have a tattoo, yours seems the best.
>
> *Peter:*   Yeah, well … thanks! Right now, I'm far away from it, but
> who knows; I will dare one day.

In most cases, the choice for a symbol will nevertheless be much more in
relation to the actual goal. Not all clients have the same way of processing
their choice. Some are just less talkative, which is just as fine.

In Ron's case – the young man you've already met before in the chapter
about step 1 – it's evident how valuable it can be to explore more deeply the
significance of the chosen symbol. Asking the right questions and showing
genuine interest often help the client become aware of deeper, additional
information about sources of motivation. Such an example as Ron's indicates that the process can be fairly straightforward, without prolonged and
intensive coaching.

Here is now something that appears to be true for people of all ages and
not just young Mission Possible clients: once they take responsibility for
both their problems and the solutions, they become autonomously motivated. The coach only guides the process, literally from 'one step behind the
shoulder'. With a robust support system in place and a well-chosen symbol
to maximize motivation, the client is able to keep himself on track.

A case study from practice: Ron continuation

Let's look further at how Ron's getting on.

Ron has a certain advantage because he already has a hero: Jamie
Oliver. Even before starting his Mission Possible-program, Jamie was
Ron's symbol of success as well as of his love of cooking.

By getting Ron to talk more about why he admires Jamie so much, he
soon reveals that talents and qualities he ascribes to Jamie are ones that
he can actually recognize in himself. Ron may only be vaguely aware
of latent skills that are deeply hidden yet present. They're skills he certainly wants to develop and learn more about. In this way, qualities
that reveal themselves during the meeting automatically become part
of Ron's Mission Possible-program. In fact, Ron unconsciously projects
all these traits, skills, and experiences that he describes as belonging to
Jamie, on himself.

Daring to dream

It begins as a secretly fostered dream he is very hesitant to even allow
himself. But gradually, during the process, Ron begins to accept that this
dream could come true for him. Maybe *his* future will be slightly less glam-
orous than Jamie Oliver's, but at least Ron can accept that it's all right for
him to take the necessary steps to pursue a career as a professional chef.

Exploring the depth in the symbol

Jamie Oliver and his adventures continue to be the subject of a number of meetings with Ron, who opens up and talks increasingly freely about his admiration for Jamie. At the start of one meeting, Ron rushes in excitedly: he's just heard that the famous international chef is looking for 15 teenage boys and girls for a special project. Could *he* dare to dream of getting involved … and dare to apply? Ron is motivated by Jamie's pursuit of socially responsible business activities and his willingness to give young people with potentially fewer opportunities a chance to work in his restaurant Fifteen. This aspect of Jamie's socially engaged entrepreneurship is particularly touching for Ron. It makes him question and look more closely at the fact that he was adopted as a baby. He becomes more aware of the extent to which it occupies his thoughts, something he had until now tended to push away into the background. Now he gradually comes to know that he wants to do something really meaningful to help those in society who are less fortunate, just as he once was.

Time passes, and Ron successfully completes his Mission Possible-program. Two years of catering training later, Ron, now almost 20 years old and armed with his first diploma, goes off to work in Sri Lanka for 10 months. There he supports a charity running an orphanage; together with a group of young people, he does all he can to improve the circumstances of the children living there.

He regularly posts items on his vlog-diary and is obviously having the time of his life. It is clear that he has gained considerable insight into the effects of poverty on the people there. He also writes that he now understands better why women are sometimes simply unable to look after and provide for their children themselves.

With just three months of his contract still to go before he travels back home, he says that he has already enrolled for the next stage of his catering training, adding, "I'm really looking forward to it!" He also reveals that he's very excited about traveling more: "Maybe I can combine travel and work later on. I have certainly developed an appetite for more."

Step 5: Trust and self-confidence

Trust, having a confident and positive outlook for the future, is one of the most important sources of motivation any person needs to be able to work toward realizing such a future. If a task is to be completed with any reasonable degree of success, then it is essential that positive expectations are the foundation of all serious efforts. Put another way, there's very little hope that all will turn out well without at least *some* trust. Without that minimum of trust, problems remain just problems instead of matters that can be dealt with and resolved. Hope, combined with the expectation of a positive outcome, is the key to perceiving a problem as an opportunity. For many young people, their life experiences already have made this a considerable challenge, which is why step 5 is solely designed to regain and further develop trust and self-confidence.

A list of reasons for optimism

At least one of the meetings with your client centers around making as long a list as possible of reasons for being optimistic, with questions such as these:

"What reasons do you have for believing that you can reach your goal?"
"What makes you feel confident about yourself?"

If your client has trouble in answering questions on this topic – which is all too often the case, especially in the beginning – then this interview with you will turn out to be a significant source of new discoveries.

After all, one of the prime reasons a client turns to a coach for help is that he finds himself stuck somewhere in his development. From such a state of mind, the paralyzing despair of being unable to find a way out on their own is often dominating for the client. No wonder, then, that the answer "No idea!" is so common before the conversation even gets properly under way.

Staying relaxed, patient yet alert, and with the gentle persistence to ask more in-depth questions is the best and only option to keep the exchange going. In this way, by asking trust-specific, and 'best-hope' questions, you can help your client to regain an optimistic view of his future. Questions about exceptions to the problem or experiences with previously successfully solved problems offer solutions. Questions like these help the coach to move the client gently in the right direction:

> "What situations can you mention where your problem doesn't occur or is at least less present?"
> "What problems have you ever before in your life already solved?"
> "How did you manage to do that? What worked in that particular situation?"
> "Considering what worked before, what do you think you need to do now in order to be successful this time too?"
> "How could your previous successes in problem solving help you in this situation too? What reasons do you have to be optimistic about achieving your goal?"
> "What will other people say when asked why they trust you can do it? What will they mention as good reasons for trusting you to achieve your goal?"
> "What will your parents/family/brothers/sisters/uncles/friends/teachers say if you ask them?"
> "Is there anything else you can think of?"

These are just a few sample questions to help you move your client beyond the "I've no idea!" stage, and that will almost certainly elicit more response than just that. If you feel your client's list is still rather short, it's easy enough to ask him if he'd like some help. Of course, it goes without saying that you try to abstain from immediately giving suggestions.

> "Just take your time. I know my questions can be difficult to answer. They take time to contemplate and formulate an answer. How would you feel about a little help, and we explore the questions together?"

If the client – in this case – agrees to let you help him, then the conversation may go somewhat like this:

> "I can see that you really want to go for it! Y'know, willpower is a very powerful instrument of change. It's a quality, a character trait, that not everybody possesses to the same extent, but you have already proven to me that you've got what it takes and are very determined."
>
> Or:
>
> "I can see that you're taking your time to really think about this question. That's beautiful. It's quite necessary to think things over thoroughly when important decisions are involved."

Changing perspectives

Asking the same question but using different words and a different perspective can be most effective in situations in which a client is experiencing some difficulty in answering. Maybe it's enough just to ask more indirectly or to split the question into smaller portions. The goal at this point is to create a list of reasons he and others should believe in his ability to achieve his goal. Asking explicitly about qualities, traits, skills, and practical experience is a way to expand the list. Analyzing previous successes at problem solving is especially powerful as a source of building self-confidence. In fact, this is the only situation in a Solution Focused approach in which analyzing proves to be helpful and can even be of vital importance.

Long-term effect

The key is to determine all possible resources that increase the client's confidence in his ability to achieve his goal and help him to become consciously aware of them. Only this conscious awareness of his resources can help your client apply them in future situations too. This way, your client will not only find solutions and achieve goals in this present situation with you as his coach by his side, but he will also learn to do the same independently in the future.

What qualifies as a 'good' reason?

Everything and anything that empowers your client's belief in a successful conclusion to the program is, in principle, useful. Even the client's statement – "Just because *I* want it!" or "I just *know*!" – can work wonders. In fact, all possible internal and external resources (this subject will be explored more fully in the next chapter on step 6) are acceptable and useful reasons to be optimistic, as long as they help the client believe in a positive result. Every reason that strengthens the idea that the goal *can* be reached is a good enough reason and helps to fuel a growing sense of self-confidence.

Discovering why others believe in a successful outcome

Optimism and motivation expand as adolescents realize that other people believe in them and have confidence in them. The more supporters and other significant people around them believe in them and have confidence in their achievements, the more they start to believe in themselves. In some cases, such trust and confidence of the environment is naturally present, and the involvement is expressed in word and deed. But all too often, the degree of this trust and confidence is more subtle and implicit. In those cases, the environment seems to think that their confidence and support are obvious, but it is never really vocalized. If you are dealing with a client who has doubts about the trust of others, a direct question helps to provide clarity.

> "What, do you think, makes your friends and/or family members (your supporters) confident that you will successfully reach your goal?"

This direct question helps the client to put himself in other people's shoes, looking at him from their point of view. At the same time, it's a way of getting him to get used to the idea of going out and asking this same question of those in his network. In this way, a positive dialogue is initiated between the client and his environment. It's a chance to replace old patterns of expectations with new ones. This question also helps to bring up unresolved conflicts or old pain by changing the perspective in a positive way.

Doing what works

For some people   and not just the adolescents that are the target group of this book and the Mission Possible-program – it's very hard, even impossible, to do this exercise, that is, to mentally put themselves in other people's shoes. This is especially the case with those in a specific part of the so-called autistic spectrum: a question about what they think others think of them can be totally fruitless. If this is so, the coach just has to ignore this line of questioning, limiting it to getting the client to go around asking people directly why they have confidence in him. The client can do this himself or use a letter that you help him to compose; he can even use a sort of questionnaire containing all the relevant questions. Above all, it's important that the coach remains flexible and creative so the client can act independently as much as possible.

The power of compliments

Self-confidence doesn't just happen all by itself; it is a quality that *develops* and grows with time. Confidence in personal qualities and skills results from having had a sufficient number of positive experiences. Negative experiences undermine self-confidence, especially if they are numerous. A strong inner critic (the superego or Über Ich, according to S. Freud and C. Jung) can be equally destructive. For someone with little self-confidence, it can be hard even to observe and label good experiences as actually positive! When the voice of the inner has strong negative opinions self-confidence is under pressure 24/7.

Young people in particular are at an age when their inner critic works overtime. After all, these young people are busy finding their place in the world and look critically at themselves in relation to others. They're going through a life phase when peer pressure is at its peak. "Who's in and who's not?" is a theme that seems to be the main focus of their concerns.

Using compliments in coaching adolescents

Certainly, also adolescents need encouragement and compliments to build healthy self-confidence. Unfortunately, stacking up a lot of appreciation and compliments is no guarantee for extra self-confidence or a healthy self-image. So, what to do then? And how? How do you as a coach appreciate your client without triggering his inner critic, and accidently creating lower self-esteem? How do you create a positive validation at the right time and dosage, that doesn't create an adverse reaction? The answer is not easily given. First, always show your client that you are proud of him for his efforts. However, do not place him on a pedestal as Superman if you know in your heart that this is not the whole truth. Young people are sensitive and perceptive and will pick up on these inconsistencies.

Fitting like a glove

It's part of the coach's job to help his client spot and welcome the positive events in his life, as well as to support him in experiencing things as positive. Above all, it's important to help the client go beyond the boundaries of negative conditioning in order to enjoy all the positive things in life so that his self-confidence can grow.

Compliments are a powerful tool at this stage, especially when used wisely. This raises two important questions: "What qualifies as a 'good' compliment?" and "What makes a compliment really effective?"

Making a compliment in the 'right' way means giving the exactly appropriate dose (not too much!), given at the 'right' time, being relevant and absolutely sincere. Only compliments that meet these requirements get value:

- the right moment (timing)
- the right amount (not too much!)
- relevance (context)
- sincerity (honest)
- above all, the right wording (nonjudgmental).

With all such elements, a compliment becomes valuable and effective, contributing gently but clearly to the client's developing self-confidence and healthy self-image. A carefully worded compliment at the right moment can help the client become more aware of the true value of all his efforts in achieving the result that the compliment is about.

If a compliment complies with these criteria, it's simply a straightforward compliment that makes the client feel seen and appreciated. This alone is positive and uplifting! A sufficient number of such experiences will almost certainly help build self-confidence. But much more can be achieved with a compliment.

Empowering compliments

It's possible to enhance the value of a compliment by giving it in three stages. It becomes more than just an appreciation that the client is given. It's possible to use compliments to create a moment of reflection so that the client truly realizes how he has successfully used his own resources.

In his book on Kids'Skills, Ben Furman specifically calls this 'three-stage compliment' the 'triple-praise compliment'. This is a way of giving a compliment that expresses:

- exclamation of appreciation (Wow!)
- showing interest (How did you do that?)
- understanding of the difficulty of the performed task (That must have been really hard.)
- asking the recipient's advice, help or explanation, by specifically asking after the used (inner)resources (Show me how you did that? Can you teach me?)
- another exclamation of appreciation (Fantastic!)

Compliments are an essential part of any Solution Focused approach. Recognizing and stating the difficulty of the problem and positively confirming what a client is already doing well encourages and motivates change. At the same time, your client feels your involvement and understanding, which in itself is an encouragement. Compliments increase what goes well. Moreover, helping your client to think about how other people involved would compliment him, changing perspective, connects him with the most important people in his life outside your consulting room.

Negative effects

Yet recent scientific research shows that giving compliments also can have adverse effects. For example, someone can become fearful of failure by being complimented too much. After all, on the next occasion, he wants to be able to meet that same expectation again. In that way, even given with good intentions, receiving compliments increases stress in new situations.

Compliments given at identity level, such as 'you are sweet, beautiful, handsome, or smart' and so on, prove not to be very useful either. They only confirm a certain aspect of the personality that the recipient himself has little influence on. In a Solution Focused approach, therefore, consistent to 'doing what works', it's wise to apply compliments in moderation and, in particular, to keep them process-oriented.

A case study from practice: Luc's 'triple-praise' compliment

Luc (17) has just made a difficult decision. After considerable hesitation, he has finally told his teacher that his 16-year-old sister, Laura, has recently started dating a boy in a higher class – a boy with a bad reputation who is said to have criminal associations. In general, Luc is very loyal and discrete in his dealings with friends as well as with his sister. But in this case, he feels a responsibility to let the teacher know about this current situation. Although he is sure Laura wouldn't want him to talk about it and he certainly doesn't want to put his sister's friendship under any pressure, he still feels he must talk to the teacher. He insists immediately that the information they share must be treated as absolutely confidential.

Luc is very fond of Laura and certainly wishes her no harm, either from her unsuitable boyfriend or by any indiscretion of his in sharing what he knows with the teacher. For more than a week, it's been troubling him, and in the end, the only solution he could think of was to talk confidentially with someone in authority. He initially considered talking with Laura but let go of that idea when he realized that she probably knew nothing of her boyfriend's assumed criminal background, and he didn't want to scare her in any way.

The teacher, Mr. Robins, pays full attention to Luc as he explains what's happening. He is rather shocked by what he hears and is very concerned about Laura. He is already aware of the reputation of the boy in question. When Luc finishes, Mr. Robins first compliments him.

Mr. Robins: Luc, thank you for trusting me with this information. It must have been pretty hard for you ... and it's clear that you've really thought a lot about it. May I ask what led you in the end to come and talk to me?

Luc: I'm pretty sure that Laura just doesn't know about this boy's background, and I don't want to scare her. I mean, you know her and what she's like, and I wouldn't want anything unpleasant to happen to her.

Mr. Robins: Have you any idea what enabled you to weigh up all the different aspects of this situation so well?

Luc: Well ... I'd feel pretty guilty if anything should happen to Laura. And I just took all the time I needed in order to

Mr. Robins:

think things over really well. I didn't want to rush things. What I actually wanted to do was to fix this (bad name) once and for all. You know, he's even been telling nasty lies about her – I heard this from a friend who sometimes cycles home with him. But I wanted to think things through properly, and that's when I decided to talk to you, Mr. Robins. After all, we've often had a good chat together, at sport and at school, and because you also know my sister.

Mr. Robins: Well, well, Luc ... what a story! It's perfectly clear that you really have looked at all sides of this situation very carefully. You've proven yourself to be very responsible and grown up in how you've dealt with all this. I'm very pleased with you. By the way, it would really help me if I could talk with your mother and, yes, also with Laura. I'm pretty certain that even though it might be difficult for her at first, she'll be happy to know that her brother cares so much for her. What do you think? Anyway, I'm proud of you, Luc!

The 'gossip compliment'

The teacher, Mr. Robins, asks Luc for his permission to first discuss the current situation with his mother. Although Luc clearly is not too happy with the idea, he understands that the teacher must now take action and so gives his approval. The teacher picks up the phone and calls the number that Luc provides him. Luckily, Luc's mother picks up the phone. The teacher explains who he is and why he is calling and goes on to say that he has just had a worthwhile talk with her son Luc. He also tells her how impressed he is with Luc's mature behavior and responsible nature. "You can rightly be proud of your son, Mrs. Baxter," he says, allaying any concerns the mother may initially have had about being called by Luc's teacher. Since Luc is of course listening, he hears once again – but indirectly now – the appreciation for and recognition of his actions.

Appreciation

In this anecdote, it is clear to Luc at the end of the meeting the extent of Mr. Robins's appreciation for Luc's decision; he also knows which of his personal qualities were involved in reaching this decision. When his teacher also mentions what Luc's sister would think of what he has done, he adds value to the compliment as well as reassuring Luc about his relationship with his sister Laura.

Effective

Indirect compliments, both 'through-others' and 'gossip', are extremely effective ways of complimenting young people. The recipient is present and is allowed to 'overhear' the compliment that is described to someone else. Such compliments, which need to be expressed with considerable subtlety, serve to support and confirm existing relationships that are important to the young person in question. There's an additional advantage to this sort of compliment: a compliment given directly is all too often harder to accept than when given in this roundabout way to a significant person in the recipient's life.

Slowly and gently

As mentioned earlier, a number of conditions must be met to ensure the full value and effect of a compliment, all requiring precise timing. It is crucial *not* to overdo things. Young people are very sensitive when it comes to exaggeration and insincere flattery. What works best is to start carefully and to observe how the compliment is received. 'Dip your toe in the water before jumping in' perfectly describes the safest approach! Experience will soon make clear what sort of compliment works best with each individual.

Giving and receiving

It's a matter of being prepared to *practice*. The nice thing about practicing giving compliments is that it is mostly fun to do. After all, compliments are generally received with some degree of pleasure. It's no wonder, then, that it's highly agreeable to be generous in giving compliments while at the same time becoming increasingly skilled in this important form of communication. There's yet another advantage to *giving* compliments: the openness and friendly warmth of the contact at that moment increases the chance of *receiving* compliments! In other words, a small investment can reap generous rewards.

Indirect

By far the most pleasant way to compliment someone is when no *explicit* compliment is required before the recipient feels appreciated and validated in his competence. An example of such a compliment follows, in the section 'Perfect compliment'. Such a compliment can be seen as empowering, a way to strengthen autonomy. This remarkably subtle way of expressing appreciation and validation gives the recipient plenty of space to make his own interpretation, independent of the opinion of the giver. As the example indicates, this style requires some skills, like attention, timing, and above all, creativity. I heard the following excellent example of an autonomy-enforcing compliment from a mother, who herself was the daughter of perhaps the most famous psychotherapist of the last century, Milton H. Erickson. This is the specialist who is viewed as the founder of the Solution Focused approach.

Perfect compliment

This story I heard directly from Betty Alice Erickson is an example of one of the finest compliments that could be given. It involves her two sons, who grew up at the time her father, Dr. Milton Erickson, was already quite advanced in years. One day, Erickson is sitting in his wheelchair in the garden, enjoying the sun and his grandchildren. David, then 9 years old, pulls up some of the carrots he's been growing in the vegetable garden. Very satisfied with his carrots, he runs over to Erickson and gives him one. "Look, Grandpa – this comes out of *my* garden!" Erickson takes the carrot in his lean hands and studies it in silence. He turns the carrot this way and that before saying slowly to his grandson, "It's certainly very orange." David, feeling encouraged, adds: "Yes, Grandpa, and *I* grew it!" Erickson doesn't respond but continues to stare at the carrot. "It's extremely straight," he declares. "Yes, Grandpa, and *I* grew it!" David repeats with increasing enthusiasm. "Hmmm," says Erickson, "it's also pretty big." "Yes, Grandpa. *I* made it grow! It grew in *my* garden," David repeats insistently.

Erickson seems unmoved by his grandson's enthusiasm and continues to stare at the carrot in his hand. After a while, he says, "I bet it tastes delicious." David is now totally delighted, jumping up and down excitedly, dancing around his grandfather's wheelchair and calling out, "*I* grew it, Grandpa!"

Impatient at the lack of further response, he grabs the carrot out of Erickson's hand, rushes off to pull up the remaining carrots, and runs to the back door of the house, where his mother has just appeared. "Look, Mum, these are my very own carrots that *I* grew, and Grandpa says that I've grown the best carrots in the whole world!"

Subtle = effective

This example of a subtle compliment, neutrally naming all characteristics, contains all the features that make such a compliment so effective. In effect, it is the *child* who expresses the compliment, in his own words and founded on his own sense of competence and autonomy. David's expression is totally independent of any appreciation by someone else (in this case, his grandfather).

Consider for a moment how different it would have been if Erickson had simply said, "You grow the best carrots in the world!" Imagine how David would have felt if the *next* carrot had provoked a different response. After all, carrots have the natural tendency to be inconsistent in their form. Then David could have felt disappointed or even that he had in some way failed. Then, too, an expectation may have arisen, such that each carrot that was different (not 'very long', not 'remarkably orange') could have made David feel that he had somehow failed. And *that* is certainly not the intention of a compliment!

In the light of this, it's perhaps salutary to consider what the effect is of repeatedly praising a child with words like "Aren't you a clever little boy!"

Tools for the toolbox

Features that contribute to the effectiveness of a compliment:

- Appreciation – "I feel appreciated."
- Recognition – "I feel seen."
- Interest – "I am worthwhile."
- Sincerity (nonverbal) – "He means what he says."
- Subtle invitation to do more of the same – "I'm going to do this more often."
- Motivation – "It works, so I want more. I'll do more."
- Supporting skills – "I can do it!"
- Clear and detailed – "I know exactly what I've done well."
- Relevancy, being to the point – "I understand it."
- Stimulating autonomy – "I can do it by myself, without any help."
- (Preferably) focused on the behavior or process – "I am independent."
- Without any pressure to perform – "I may ..."
- Just the right amount – not exaggerated but perfectly tailored to the situation

Step 6: Resources: reasons to be optimistic

This step in the Mission Possible-program specifically involves the internal resources that your client already possesses. Put another way, resources are anything that can be put to use to resolve a problem. These are the means that, broadly speaking, can be implemented in a positive way to shift the problem in the direction of a solution. Such resources include character traits, talents, skills, knowledge, experience (both positive and negative), insights, and intuitions, all of which contribute constructively to bringing the preferred goal closer. Indeed, previous negative experiences can also be a resource, indicating what no longer needs to be experienced as well as what someone no longer *wants* to experience – he has *learned* from that experience.

Discovering individual internal resources

It is unfortunate that it is precisely such valuable resources that young people often have trouble recalling in times of stress, when they're dealing with problems. The resources are definitely there, but they appear to be locked away and seem inaccessible at that moment. They are either invisible or are viewed through a filter tainted by negative beliefs and feelings around the problem. Nevertheless, these resources are of crucial importance and need to be made available in order to achieve the desired result of solving a problem. Such resources provide essential leverage to start moving toward the goal.

External resources

Apart from *internal* resources, such as character traits, talents, skills, knowledge, experience, insights, and intuition, there are also, of course, *external* resources. These consist amongst others of: friends, family, other significant people in your client's life, other people's experiences, exceptions to the problems, support systems (mentors, family coaches, social workers, and suchlike), and local positive, supportive environmental factors (such as a community center, sports and recreation facilities, nature, etc.). Put more simply, these external resources are resources for which a young person needs other people or things from outside. However, he can only partially influence these external resources. And although they are extremely important in the client's process, it is primarily the internal resources that are the focus of this Mission Possible step.

These resources aren't always so obvious. A trait or feeling that initially may appear negative or seem useless may later turn out to be a valuable resource when perceived from another point of view.

A case study from school

> *Student:*   I am *really* angry about what has happened again in the group. This is the third time this week that I've got so angry about the group
>
> *Teacher:*   Annabel, it's clear that you take these things very seriously. I can appreciate just how involved you are with the group. I'm impressed by the extent to which such things matter to you. You don't give up but keep addressing the problem. I wish everyone were as involved and concerned as you.

Reframing

In this case study, the teacher reframes the perceptions of the student, providing a positive appreciation of what at first glance appears negative, turning the evident irritation of the student into a useful resource. Getting involved is indeed a positive quality. In the Solution Focused approach, the first rule is 'to do more of what works'. While there is initially nothing useful about the student's anger, reframing can help her to see new possibilities.

Expanding vision

When working with young people, it's fairly common that emotions are expressed in ways that block the availability of the inherent resources. It would then be appropriate to say that they get stuck in a 'fixed mindset'. The running emotions form a barrier to growth. It is, however, possible to create the necessary space to learn and grow. Paying close attention and reframing what is observed will help reveal the underlying positive intentions of the behavior. Furthermore, it can help to introduce 'differentiation': from just black and white to the many shades of grey in between. Young people tend to be rather black and white in their way of perceiving things. A well-placed and mature reframing of what is perceived can be most helpful to stop and turn the emotional tide.

Reframing – mirroring information provided by the client but reflected in a more positive form – is an important item in your toolkit as coach. By reframing consistently, it's possible to influence positively the tone of the exchange as well as the key message.

Various forms of reframing include:

1   *from negative to positive;*

    (You're insolent → You dare to stand up for yourself)

2   *from an unchangeable personality trait to a quality that's related to a specific situation;*

    (I was being stupid → I behaved unwisely)

3   *from permanent to temporary;*

    (I never succeed → I'm currently not yet successful)

4   *from an external factor that cannot be influenced to one that can be influenced;*

    (He's always on my case → I somehow seem to carry the blame)

5   *from a complaint to a wish;*

    (I'm really annoyed about this → I want this to change)

Increasing awareness and self-confidence

As is clear from previous chapters, all steps in the Mission Possible-program are designed to reinforce and expand self-confidence. The more confident your client is, the greater his motivation to *want* to work toward the preferred goals and to genuinely reach them. That is why all the steps are primarily focused on the process of awareness – of personal potential, internal and external resources, previous successes, and possible benefits as well as developing a clear picture of the preferred outcomes. *All of this is latently present.* That is a precondition for working with Mission Possible. It is this assumption that makes it possible for the client to take the helm. Self-determination and self-regulation are paramount. The process and the outcomes are all his. In the end, he knows better than anyone else which possibilities he has or can acquire in order to work toward his goals. However, at the start of the process, he usually isn't fully aware of the possibilities at hand.

Growing self-confidence

Because the steps in the Mission Possible-program are designed to fuel the process of growing awareness, the possibilities available to your client become more visible as he progresses. Naturally, from the moment the possibilities are seen and recognized, they can then be implemented – with awareness *and* an increasing sense of competence. As competence grows, so too does the client's self-confidence: "I *can* do it! And I can do it by myself, even if my coach guides me a bit."

Slowly but surely, then, a positive cycle develops while working with the Mission Possible steps:

- thinking about goals and perspectives;
- investigating current progress and analyzing previous successes;
- finding affirming explanations;
- appreciating and feeling competent;
- developing a positive attitude and mindset (growth-mindset);
- being willing to cooperate;
- generating many creative ideas on the way to solutions;
- analyzing and understanding progress;
- getting more validation, appreciation ... and so on.

Awareness provides insight. Insight provides a perspective on growth and development. A perspective on development nourishes (self-)confidence and hope. Confidence and hope fuel the essential motivation to take action.

Step 7: Scaling

Questions that result in answers involving scaling are perhaps the most characteristic and best-known intervention in the Solution Focused approach. Scaling is discussed in detail in the chapter about Step 7 in the Mission Possible workbook.

The scaling question was originally created in the 1970s by Steve de Shazer as a way of getting clarity about a client's perception of his progress. But since then, many useful variations have been developed.

And there's a good reason for this: to my knowledge, there are very few interventions that are as applicable, useful, creative, and effective as scaling questions. Howsoever you use it, the scaling question is a powerful tool in a wide variety of situations, with varying purposes and results. Scaling is an easy way of putting progress toward the main goal into perspective. Besides, at the start of a process, it's an agreeable way of measuring the client's starting position in relation to the preferred goal. And you can achieve a great deal more with this remarkable sort of question.

Flexibility

The scaling question is applicable for various purposes and timing. At part of the start of a Mission Possible process, and later, too, repeating the scaling question (as a regular part of each meeting) can be a valuable way of monitoring progress. Apart from this, you can vary the focus of the scaling question. For example, you want to measure the quality of motivation:

> "On a scale from 0 to 10, how motivated do you feel about achieving your goal? Where 0 means you're totally unmotivated and 10 means you just can't wait to get to work ..."

Such different goals can all present themselves at different moments during the Mission Possible process. Practically, this means that it's quite common to pose scaling questions more often in different phases of a Mission Possible process.

Monitor progress

The most common form of the scaling question is to monitor progress on the way to the preferred goal. Together with the client, you determine the initial or current position (see the diagram later in this chapter). You can draw this simple scaling question as a straight line on a piece of paper, but there's plenty of room for your own creativity in how you employ scaling. Yes, a straightforward pen and paper are fine, but a staircase, a rocket, walking along a path, or climbing an actual climbing wall are all useful metaphors to use as scaling tools.

Fun

During a coaching session with young children and teenagers, it's especially effective as well as fun to combine the scaling question with some form of physical activity. It's a great way to be active together! Imagine, then, laying out the scale on the floor. Post-its or colored cards are ideal for writing the numbers on. And there are plenty of ready-made scaling tools on the market with numbers 0 to 10 in the form of large footsteps, colored circles, or strings – it makes no difference what tool you use in order to get the required result. What remains important is that the client fully understands that it's more than 'just giving a number or grade' but that scaling is a method that helps him on his way to his goal. It's for this reason that in my own practice, I never talk about 'giving a number' when I ask the scaling question; rather,

I always talk about where the client *is* or wants to go *to*. The scale represents a path, a journey toward a certain destiny.

Physical distance

In the event you've laid out a scale on the floor and then asked your young client to walk along the scale with you, it's important to remember that your physical presence can influence him. That's why you must carefully choose where you stand, sometimes literally one step behind *and* respecting the client's 'intimate space'. Every person has an individual need for appropriate personal distance. Stand neither too close nor too far away.

If you stand too close your client, who is often smaller or younger than you, he might feel intimidated. Too far, and you will lose valuable contact. *Please note that there is no standard definition for what is the 'right' distance.* This is a matter of being observant and feeling what is right for *this* client.

Language

Physically walking the scale adds an extra benefit for your client. It gives the scaling question a less mental dimension, enhancing the chance that the client has a broader sensory perception of the answer, and actually *feels* what is his right spot. *All* nuances of language, including nonverbal aspects, provide extra opportunities to intensify and deepen the experience of the client. Making full use of all the possibilities of scaling questions requires some practice on the coach's side but is remarkably fruitful and worthwhile.

Mastering skills

Combining different, typically Solution Focused tools in one and the same powerful intervention is a challenge that requires your creativity, courage, and experience as a coach. The old saying 'practice makes perfect' is certainly true in this case! It may take you some time before you master it and feel comfortable with these tools. It will take practice to find your own particular synthesis that works well for you. Until you master these skills, it's better to keep it simple and stick to a strict and simple learning frame. Otherwise, it might feel uncomfortable for both you and your client.

For example

Here's a simple scaling frame: "This is a scale – showing a line starting at 0 and ending at 10. It represents the way from your problem to your goal. If 0 represents you haven't started yet, and 10 means that you've reached your goal, where would you place yourself now?" This simple sequence of questions will always provide you with valuable information without leading you or your young client into treacherous pitfalls.

But if, however, you succeed and cooperatively manage to explore the path to the preferred future with this powerful exercise, it is one of the most interesting and effective interventions. Most often during this exercise, the client finds his truly autonomous motivation, taking full ownership and consciously connecting with the preferred goal. This last point is even more the case when you, as the coach, are able to explore all levels (that is, the logical levels as described in NLP by Dilts and Bateson) while asking the miracle question (S. de Shazer & I.K. Berg), such as:

- *environments, external factors*

  Where are you? What's the weather like today? What are you wearing? Who do you meet? How do others respond to you? What changes can they see in you? What changes can *I* see in you?

- *behaviors*

  How do you behave? What are you doing differently?

- *capabilities or competences*

  What skills do you use? Which personality traits do you use to your advantage?

- *values and beliefs*

  What are you thinking about? What is your opinion about that?

- *identity*

  Who are you in this situation? What role do you play?

- *purpose or spirituality*

  If there is something bigger, greater than you, what *is* that? What greater purpose does it serve?

- *feelings*

  And, although not belonging to the logical levels of thinking by Dilts and Bateson, also remember to inquire after particular *feelings*. How do you feel? What does it feel like to reach your goal? What changes do you feel in your body as you have reached your goal?

Limited time span

It is, of course, unnecessary to always ask all of these questions. By listening closely to the client's answers when you ask a miracle question, it will become clear what is relevant to his process. When you pay close attention to the client's body language, you will know what to pursue further or what is 'off limits' at that moment. Timing is of the essence. The coach needs to remember that the scaling process must not take too long. A proficient coach adjusts the complexity, the number of questions, and the time involved to the client's attention span.

Key rules

To help you as a coach to set up a clear learning structure for your client while scaling, you need to remember seven golden rules:

1   Be respectful.
2   Create a clear structure of questioning for optimal learning.
3   Accept every answer you get and go with the flow of what the client presents.
4   Appreciate whatever is presented and let go of any preconditioned ideas.
5   Look for differences and nuances.
6   Be patient, bite your tongue, and count to 20 before moving on.
7   Be willing to round off the session after 10 to 15 minutes unless the client is nicely in flow and it would be a pity to interrupt.

Powerful combining

Mission Possible steps, scaling questions, and miracle questions are in themselves powerful interventions. But by combining them, an added value is created. Imagine a young client who has not yet formulated his goal with satisfactory clarity or is not yet fully a 'client' for change using this self-development program. In this case, a combination of scaling (step 7), the step involving resources (step 6), *and* the miracle question could help him get in touch at a deeper level with both his personal motivation and his preferred goal. Such a combination often elicits comments such as "I had no idea I wanted it so badly" or "Only now is it really clear to me what I truly want."

All too often, the tears, long held back, flow freely when exploring the 10 on the scale with an extended version of the miracle question. And these are tears that the client has worked hard for. They seldom need to be talked about in depth but should certainly be welcomed and given all the space they deserve. That's when your silence and full attention are the right actions.

Light hypnosis

After having felt such intense contact with his goal, often with closed eyes, the client needs a moment to come back to reality. This extended version of the miracle question frequently creates a certain hypnotic state, so your attention and guidance as coach are generally required. It's up to you to ask in a calm, soft voice if everything has been said that needs to be said, gently bringing the client back to the present moment. You'll help him by inviting him to take a few deep breaths, open his eyes (if closed), and then slowly turn around and return to the position where he started. This is now your chance to watch your client's responses attentively; more about this point follows later in the chapter about scaling technique.

Value of scaling

An important reason for implementing scaling questions is to boost self-confidence and trust in the ability to achieve the goal. It is perfectly reasonable to use scaling questions precisely when your client expresses his lack of confidence:

> "If 0 is where you have no confidence at all and 10 is where you're totally convinced you can reach your goal, where are you now on this scale?"

Discovering that a lot has already been achieved and that there are still plenty of possibilities is excellent support for anybody's confidence, not just for adolescents. This scale introduces hope and nuances in the black-and-white world of young people, who are often struggling with the issue of their (self-)confidence and self-esteem. By building self-confidence and providing a perspective of becoming even more confident, you help your young client to find the motivation to take action.

Tool for change

Equally well, someone who feels totally indifferent to everything has no reason to make any changes or to take any action.

The scaling process described here is a powerful tool to facilitate taking concrete steps toward change.

You can also use scaling to help your client determine when he can proceed independently, at which point you withdraw to the background. After all, a goal does not have to be completely achieved before the client starts managing on his own. As soon as he is able to work self-sufficiently toward his goals, further coaching is no longer so necessary. This is a realistic way of supporting the client's independence.

Keeping an eye on progress

As already mentioned, being aware of existing resources is vitally important for developing self-confidence. However, there is more to expanding available resources than helping the client become aware of his qualities and personality traits. Equally important is the extent to which he is able to perceive his progress and the first signs of success on the way to his goal.

By constantly keeping an eye on what he has already achieved in each subsequent step, however minor, is a fresh contribution to his increasing sense of competence ... Which in turn contributes to his increasingly positive self-image.

Repetition

There are numerous ways to measure progress and to develop awareness. Scaling, just one of those many ways, is indispensable in the Mission Possible-program. It is so essential that it's advisable to repeat it several times during the client's process. When scaling with different goals and at different moments, you actually help your client to gain both a clear picture of his progress and successes, as well as providing a distinct boost to his self-confidence. After all, he then sees clearly how his skills are growing and how competent he is becoming! And this, in turn, fuels his motivation, helps keep him motivated, and nurtures his independence.

The technique of scaling

The basics of scaling conform to a fixed pattern of questions. Within this pattern, there's room for you to make variations such as emphasizing specific goals or using other Solution Focused tools. For example, the step of scaling combines perfectly with talking about the preferred future (step 1) by asking a miracle question as well as by asking questions about resources (step 6). Here's an example from practice in which the combination of these three steps works out in a wonderful way, making them all one powerful Solution Focused intervention.

A case study from practice: Sam

Sam, 18 years old, is working with his coach on defying temptation to overspend his monthly budget. He stated to want this because it is frequently getting him into trouble. His preferred future is not to owe money to either his parents or his friends. His actual goal is "being able to look at tempting things, like watches and digital gadgets in an online store, without a feeling of 'I need to have this'." When analyzing his preferred future of being debt-free, this particular part in the process was his most difficult challenge.

Sam: If I can tackle feeling tempted to actually buy, because I feel I need it, then I can bring my goal of being free of debts closer. Then I can save money to pay off my debts entirely.

Now he is two months along his path of working on this new behavior. He made some progress and has the extra savings to prove it in his bank account. But some moments of struggle with the temptations also have been part of his process. Now he is truly disappointed about his moments of weakness. He bought some really cool sneakers but found himself not enjoying having and wearing them.

Sam: They represent my failure. Every time I want to wear them, they remind me of not living up to my promises. I hear myself talking, saying to myself I am stupid and I'll never succeed in reaching my goal.

Coach: Wow, Sam, that is quite a harsh verdict you are giving yourself. What do you think you did to deserve that?

Sam: I failed. I fell through and gave in to the temptation.

Coach: How many times did that happen over the last period?

Sam: Only once.

Coach: And how many times did you succeed in fighting other temptations?

Sam: Oh, many times.

Coach: Really? Wow, tell me about it. In fact, what would you say if we make some space to do a scaling exercise, just to see where you stand today?

The coach asked Sam scaling questions on previous occasions. Therefore, Sam already knows what he can expect.

Sam: Okay. Then I would say I'm at 7 now.

Coach: Great! That's a step or two forward since last time we scaled. If I remember correctly, you placed yourself at 5 a little over a week ago. What did you do to make such a giant step in a relatively short time? What is different between being at 5 then and now being at 7?

Sam: Well, I realized when you asked this, although I failed once and bought the sneakers, there were more than 5 situations where I didn't fail and resisted all temptation.

Coach: How did you do that? That must have been really hard. What made you resist?

With this last question, the coach is inquiring after Sam's inner resources. In fact, the coach is incorporating step 6 of the Mission Possible-program (talking about inner resources) in the scaling exercise of step 7.

Sam: When I saw the ads pop up, at first, I was tempted. I thought, wow, that's cool! But immediately after, I kept looking at my thoughts. I could see how I was feeling aroused one moment and thought about my goal the next. Then I questioned myself. Do I really need this? Is this a good idea? Just like we discussed before, I kept my focus on my inner dialogue.

Coach: Wow, Sam! That's impressive! What made you able to do that?

Sam: I thought about how I really wanted to succeed. And also, I thought about my parents. You know, how they would react if I would ask them to help me out. Again!

Coach: Wow! How did that make you feel?

Sam: It made me feel strong and really wanting to persevere. I felt already ashamed by the thought of having to face them with a failure.

Coach: So it's important for you to make your parents proud of you? And just the thought of confronting them with another debt was making you think twice?

Sam: Yip. It did ... make me feel ashamed already. And I knew in that moment, I didn't want to do that anymore.

Coach: That's sounds to me like you are really taking responsibility, Sam. That's a very mature way of thinking. When did the little 'relapse' with the sneakers happen? Was that earlier or later in the week?

Sam: Right at the beginning.

Coach: What would you say, if we just make a little time lapse to being on 10? Would you be interested in exploring how it would be there?

Sam: Do you mean we would just pretend I am there already? Okay.

Coach: Good, let's explore this position, your goal, a little. If you want, you can close your eyes and just imagine it already happening.

Sam: Just like that?

Coach: Yes. Just imagine yourself having arrived. You've worked hard, and you've reached your goal of being free of debts and resisting temptations. Are you there?

Sam: Yes, I am.

Coach: How does it feel to have now reached your goal?

Sam: Fantastic! I feel relieved, like a stone has been lifted off of me.

Coach: Oh, I can understand that feels relieving. What more?

Sam: I feel happy, light in my heart.

Coach: And why is that?

Sam: Because I'm not feeling burdened by feelings of guilt and shame anymore.

Coach: Wow! That is wonderful.

Sam: Yes, it is. I feel like I'm inches taller, and I notice I can't stop smiling.

Coach: What else can I or anyone else notice about you that has changed?

Sam: I am participating more in activities with my friends. I go out more.

Coach: What else?

Sam:	My parents see me more often.
Coach:	Great. How is that?
Sam:	I'm not avoiding contact anymore. I'm not afraid anymore.
Coach:	Sam, that's fantastic!
Sam:	Yes, it is. Come to think of it ... I suddenly understand that my fear of certain things, like having discussions with my parents, made me feel so unhappy. When I feel happy and am going out and seeing friends and my family, I don't think about buying stuff. In fact, I do not go online much. I have lots of other things to do.
Coach:	Wow! That sounds to me like a very valuable insight. What do you make of what you just said?
Sam:	I feel I have a better chance to stay debt free now. If I do not create situations that make me feel bad, I do not need to. I'm breaking a circle. Sigh ... I feel awesome!
Coach:	You are, Sam! Absolutely. Do you feel we have explored this position enough now, or would you like to add anything?
Sam:	No. It's enough.
Coach:	Okay, Sam, then you can slowly open your eyes and come back here in the room again. Take your time, there's no rush.
Sam:	*[Now with his eyes open]* Ah, wow. That was awesome! I can still feel it.
Coach:	What is it exactly that you feel? Could you describe that while walking back to your original position?
Sam:	*[Walking Back]* Uh, I don't know exactly. It feels a bit weird.
Coach:	What do you mean by weird?
Sam:	Weird, like I do not want to walk back. It's like it doesn't fit anymore.
Coach:	Then what *would* fit you?
Sam:	I don't know. I'm confused. I feel more at home at 8, or even 8.5.
Coach:	Okay. Just take your time to figure out what would be your best-fitting position.
Sam:	*[Leaping back and forth between 8 and 9]* It's 8.5. That feels right. This is the correct spot.
Coach:	Great! It's official. You're at 8.5. Wow, what happened between before and now? What brought on this big transition? What's different now?

The coach asks the last question in different forms just to make sure that Sam can relate to this somewhat abstract concept of suddenly having moved up the scale.

Sam:	Different is that I have felt how painful it feels when I disappoint people I love. And how wonderful I feel when I don't have feelings

like guilt and shame. I also felt how great it is to do stuff with friends and go out, not worrying. I suddenly understood that I was creating it myself. It felt horrible to see that, and then to feel how much I actually wanted that to stop. It then became important to me. Much more important than a pair of goofy sneakers could ever be.

Fixed pattern

Scaling always begins with an invitation:

> *Coach:*   Are you willing to do a process called 'scaling' with me? or Would you like to explore your goal and where you are on that path?

Naturally, you follow up with an explanation of the how and why of this process:

> "Here on the floor, you can see a line. That line represents a path with steps from 0 to 10."

After the client agrees, you start by setting up the learning frame, explaining what the scale represents:

> "Position 0 means that nothing has yet happened. Position 10 represents your preferred future, your goal. It means – hurrah! – You've reached it!"

Personally, I prefer to start with 1, since 0 means nothing. But when a young client is willing to work toward a goal, that alone is already a step that's worth appreciating. At that moment, he's already aware of his wish to make some changes or resolve a problem. It is this awareness, or just the willingness to work toward change, that's worth at least one step on the scale. That's why I like to start the scale with position 1. Appreciating what is already there is one of the principles in the Solution Focused approach.

The next question encourages your client to determine his current position on the scale:

> "If position 1 indicates that you've just begun and 10 represents the achievement of your goal, where do you place yourself on this scale now?"

He may now go and stand on the line, and you follow him calmly as described earlier. When he finds the place at which he feels comfortable ("This is it!"), ask him to turn around and look back toward 1, the start of the path.

Question 4 involves looking together at what brought him to the point at which he currently places himself. This is where your client becomes aware of all possible resources currently at his disposal.

> "What are all the things that, up till now, have helped to get you here? What has made it possible for you to stand here on this position? What worked well for you? What else?"

The answers can include anything that contributed in *any way* to his being able to choose this place on the scale: personality traits, skills, talents, previous experience, and any external resources. It's important to note that even negative experiences can result in a positive contribution and are therefore useful as a resource. Lessons learned through previous failures are still worthwhile. Knowing what *doesn't* work is useful in this process.

You are advised to take your time here so that all possibilities, however minor they may appear, can be considered. For a young client, this can be quite a journey of discovery! He may realize just how much more has actually gone well than he initially thought was possible. In this way, Mission Possible step 6 can be integrated in the scaling process of step 7.

After dealing thoroughly with Question 4, it's time to move on to Question 5. This begins by asking the client to turn around and face position 10, the goal. There are many different ways of asking Question 5. For example, you could ask him to visualize what it would be like to stand at a higher number.

> "What would the world look like from there?"

You can do this in small steps or even ask him to imagine what it would be like to jump directly to 10. While imagining what his world would be like at position 10, you could also ask the miracle question and suggest he keep his eyes closed while answering.

It is equally useful to simply ask your client what the desired situation looks like, even if not yet a 10:

> "Imagine for a moment that you're *[number of steps]* further. What has changed for you? What are you now able to do? How will that help you? Where on the scale would you like to end up? Where could you feel satisfied?"

You can now proceed to ask Question 6, but since it's about previous successes, you can choose to ask it after Question 4, when young clients often spontaneously report that they have noticed that they're managing better than before. Question 6 delves deeper. These are all suitable and effective questions at this point:

"Have you already noticed that there are moments when everything seems to be going better? Where would you place yourself on the scale at such a moment? What's the highest position you guess you've ever reached? What worked so well then? What was different then? And what exactly did you do then?"

Observing nonverbal signs of change

After looking closely at the desired result at position 10 and exploring previous successes at the start, the logical next step is to ask your client to walk back to the place on the scale where he started out. While he walks, observe the nonverbal information he inadvertently provides. If he takes his original place confidently and without hesitation, you may conclude that this spot is right for him.

Certainly, that's not always the case. When observing the client while he is walking, a hesitation or moment of discomfort is regularly seen. Is his step resilient, and is he taking his place firm and determined, or do you observe a slight hesitation, a searching, a little wobble or a clear leaning forward? All this is information that it's important to investigate further by asking him how it is to be back here on this first spot again. Usually the answer is, relatively predictable: "Fine." And that's indeed fine if he did indeed take his place securely. But if there are any conflicting signals, something has evidently changed for him, and then it's very worth your while to probe deeper.

An example of such an exchange

Client: Weird, it definitely feels different here.

Coach: What feels different?

Client: Hmm ... No idea.

Coach: Take your time. Just feel how it is to be standing here again.

Client: It feels as if I don't belong here anymore. It feels as if I've actually made more progress.

Coach: Okay ... where do you think you should be standing now?

Client: Maybe at *[number]* ...

Coach: Go ahead and stand there. Just feel if it feels okay.

Client: Maybe half a step further ... ?

Coach: Great. Try it.

Client: Yes, this feels much better. I'm now standing at *[number]*.

Coach: What do you think has happened?

Client: I'm not quite sure. But it's as if I'm actually closer to my goal now.

Coach: Excellent! Any idea how that happened?

Client: Yes. I think I understand better why I have to do this. And I have more faith in my ability to do it. There were so many things I hadn't yet considered.

Ask the questions as neutrally as possible:

"What's it like for you to be back on this spot again?"

That's when you'll often hear answers that indicate some change in the experience. Your client will say something like 'not belonging here anymore' or 'weird' or 'no longer the right spot'. In such a case, ask him where he feels would be more appropriate and invite him to move to that spot. The new spot is usually one or more steps nearer the goal.

When the client has found his new 'right spot' and seems comfortable there, it's time to ask him to describe what's different now as compared with his original position. Generally speaking, the response makes clear that a sense of physical contact with the preferred goal and then feeling how it would be to have achieved it serves to enhance his motivation. After all, he has now gained more clarity about the goal, which has at the same time become more desirable.

Ending with a SMART agreement

Conclude this part of the exercise by asking about a small, realistic step that he could take toward his goal within a distinct time frame:

"What small step can you think of that you could take, say, within a week, that would bring you closer to your end goal? Is there anything specific you could think of?"

The more concrete the description of this new step, the better. My personal preference is to ask my client to give a SMART answer, where SMART means specific, measurable, acceptable, realistic, and time-related.

In Solution Focused work, steps or goals don't always have to be SMART, but it is my experience in working with Kids'Skills and Mission Possible that with children, teenagers, and young adults it's all too often worthwhile aiming for.

Confirming handshake

All these questions and explored positions help the client gain clarity about what he's going to do next. Precisely stating his next step provides a more solid framework for invoking new progress. Consider the value of confirming his agreement with you about this concrete next step by shaking hands on it.

Discuss what was useful

When you've finished the scaling process, discuss it briefly with your client:

"Were these scaling questions useful to you? Yes? Then what helped you the most? How could you use *that* again in the next steps toward your goal?" This will help your client to become even more aware of what is helpful for him.

Tools for the toolbox

The miracle question

"Imagine that you're asleep in bed tonight, and you dream that you've achieved your goal. And imagine that when you wake up next morning, it turns out to be true! It really happened, as if a miracle had taken place.

- What would that be like?
- What would be different for you?
- How would you feel?
- What would you do?
- What would you say, for example? Or what would you think?
- What would other people see by looking at you that is different?
- How would they react? What would they say?"

Scaling: the nuts and bolts

Looking more analytically at what happens during scaling will help you to gain greater insight into the possibilities of this tool.

It is of course an excellent idea simply to use scaling to determine the client's position at a particular moment in the program. However, as you read earlier in this chapter, there are aspects of scaling that open the way to a wide range of possible applications. Just think about the combination of looking back at previous successes and resources, looking forward, and exploring the preferred future by asking the miracle question as a way of identifying with that future as if it already is here ...

Visualizing the scaling process

Figure 4.1 provides a visual representation of the various functions of the scaling exercise.

A   Client's current position
B   Confidence and hope (reviewing all resources)

Current position

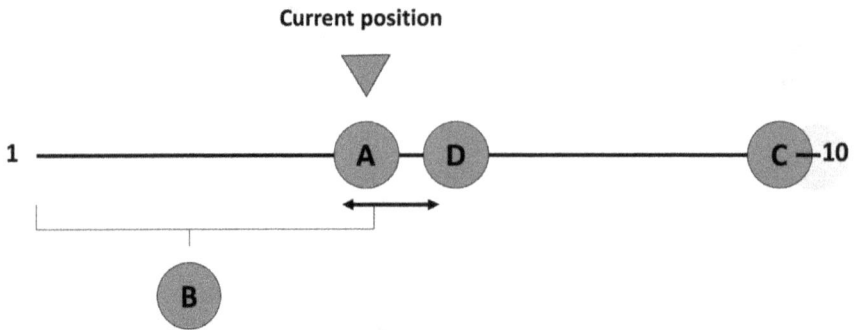

Figure 4.1 The scaling positions and their functions

C   Client's preferred position and review of consequences of reaching the goal
A–D Reviewing differences and nuances
D   Client's new position and agreeing on a small next step

In this visual, **A** represents the starting position: "On a scale from 1 to 10, if 1 is you're just starting out and 10 is your preferred outcome, where are you now?"

A represents the client's answer. Looking back toward 1 from position **A**, a clear picture of **B** becomes apparent. **B** represents everything that's already here, whatever's been achieved, learned, and experienced and has contributed to the client arriving at **A**. Becoming consciously aware of all the available resources that **B** represents serves the client as a source of hope and confidence, as well as helps him to create a more positive expectation of the future (**10**).

Focused on **10**, the preferred future, your client is able to connect more substantially with his goal. A good way to do this is by asking the miracle question or to ask more specific questions covering different aspects of the goal:

> "How would it be for you? What would be different for you? How would you feel? What would you be thinking? What would you be doing? What would other people notice about you that has changed?"

These are just some of the many possible questions you could ask that would optimize the client's connection with his goal and that help make **C** even clearer and more concrete. Answering such questions helps the client to gain a broader yet more intensive perspective of the consequences of reaching **10**.

The invitation to walk back to **A**, the starting position, sometimes results in the realization that the perception of position **A** has actually changed. It feels no longer as fitting. A *new* position **D** that now feels more relevant can be determined. Between **A** and **D**, the client becomes aware of the differences that intensely connecting with his resources and his goal, changed his perception. This new awareness often brings deeper insights and better contact on all conceivable levels. In this way, something that was previously mostly a mental construct in the client's mind can be experienced on a more emotional and physical level too. For the client it is exactly this intensified connection between these different levels of experience that opens the way and brings clarity to renew motivation and inspiration. And it is precisely this renewed motivation and inspiration that pave the way for the client to take new steps.

Now, standing at position **D**, the client can think about the next concrete step toward his goal. At that moment, it's also an opportunity to reconsider the final position at **C**. Realistically, **C** does not have to be a 'perfect 10' for everyone. Your young client can very well determine what preferred end result he will ultimately be satisfied with. 10 Is just the ideal picture, and your client's desired situation may very well be a lower number. Shifting **C** from 10 to a lower place on the scale, which may be far more practical and realistic, can be a significant source of relief and relaxation for your client.

Chapter 5

Fostering progress

It is at this point in the Mission Possible-program that the client starts taking action with all the acquired information and accrued self-confidence. Since it's totally normal that he'll be challenged at times, the steps of the Mission Possible-program are designed to support him in every possible way. They help him both to actually *take* the necessary action as well as to monitor and record (and share with all his friends and supporters!) even the most minor positive developments toward his goal. It's crucial that nothing positive is missed or ignored so that input to maintain motivation is optimized.

Step 8: Action

Thinking about a preferred future, setting goals, and the road toward achieving them is the prelude to what this Mission Possible-program is all about. It aims to help young people to bring something that seems impossible, far away, or seemingly unattainable, directly into their reach. When they create mental, physical, and emotional connections with the preferred future, taking action to realize goals becomes much easier.

Young people have every reason to postpone taking action when they experience problems, even in the face of drowning in them. Problems lead them to an area far beyond their comfort zone, where they feel independent, connected, and competent. Losing sight of the three basic needs to feel comfortable can have a paralyzing effect with emerging feelings of depression or loss of hope for improvement. Young people tend to feel overwhelmed by their problems instead of identifying them directly as a challenge and as an opportunity to learn and grow.

Build on the known

In all phases of the program, Mission Possible ensures that the client keeps in touch with his sense of independence, connectedness, and competence. In fact, the program calls upon the client to build on these fundamentals to minimize the discomfort of taking action. Action becomes a logical consequence of looking closely at a desired change – a challenge! The investment in actively working from a problem toward desired change then feels like a precalculated victory. A vital part of this victory is the client's own creation of his new horizon that, once reached, forms the basis for the next new horizon.

Action!

Taking action involves concrete agreements that must be kept. Making a list of specifically described 'next steps' is an important moment for both the coach and the client. The phase of just talking about things has come to an end; it's time for the real work to begin. By noting the agreements – perhaps in the workbook or on the flip chart – it becomes clear how and when those steps will be taken. The client knows what is expected of him, and you, the coach, know what you may expect from him. It's like a real contract.

Gathering ideas

If you look at this step in the workbook, you'll see that it's up to the client to present *his* ideas about how he could progress in small steps and in a period of time that you both agree on. Just as in Kids'Skills, it's a conscious decision to talk about *small* steps, even the smallest steps imaginable. There's a good reason for this: your young client must have the feeling that the step is achievable *and* that success is inevitable.

Challenge

Although as a coach, you always go along with what the client himself proposes, it's advisable to choose a moment to discuss steps that may be somewhat larger. After all, there is a good chance that he is perfectly capable of successfully taking a larger step. Still, it's important that he feels that he is to some extent being challenged. Otherwise, he may miss the sense of genuinely achieving something.

In the aircraft industry, technical testing of the utmost capabilities of a new design is called 'pushing the envelope'. Naturally, people are not aircraft, and not everybody has to be a highflier, but it is definitely worthwhile finding out what your client is capable of. Each new possibility that initially did not appear as such is a source of added satisfaction. Young people know this principle of expanding possibilities very well: just think about the student who gets away with arriving 10 minutes late and the next time comes 15 minutes late!

Stretching

Young people are very much in the process of discovering their potential. Therefore, it's a good idea to get them to stretch their possibilities and go exert themselves just that little bit extra. And then it is important to check whether it's a feasible step with a realistic chance of success. If either of you is in any doubt, it's better that the client takes a smaller step.

Brainstorming

At this point in the process, it sometimes happens that the client isn't immediately able to think of a step that he could take. In such an event, you are free to help him generate as many ideas as possible. A useful and fun way to help him make a choice is *divergent thinking*, a simple way of making a long list of possible steps. The key is to be light-hearted, daring to think 'out of the box,' and to be playful. As soon as lots of ideas are generated, however crazy and impractical they may seem, hope and the sense of autonomy grow. Apart from laughing a lot together, which in turn helps to generate more ideas, it's simply important to create a list; feasibility and choice of the best step to be taken come later. Ultimately it is of course up to your client to select the step that he feels is the most useful and achievable. He determines which step he wants to take and feels doable in the allotted time. Your task as coach is to follow, even if you become aware of your own impatience; after all, small steps, taken successfully, will all quickly add up to progress toward the goal. It simply means that your client will probably be ready to move on to the next stage of the process in a short time.

Intentions and promises

Your client has made his choice, so now it's up to you to make a solid agreement with him. Appropriate questions for that purpose can include:

"When are you going to do that? When do you expect to finish?"
"How are you going to practice?"
"What will I be able to see in you that will be different?"
"Will other people also be able to see the change in you?"
"And what does this change look like?"
"What precisely are you going to do?"

After talking about the various aspects of his action, it's a good idea to seal the agreement by shaking hands or some other symbolic act. Young people have all sorts of nonverbal ways of confirming agreements. If you ask him how he himself would like to confirm the agreement, you'll keep yourself up to date on the current fashion in such matters! So you, in turn, learn from your client.

Step 9: Keeping log

Change is inevitable. It's the only constant feature of our lives. Each moment, each second, each minute … not a single one is the same as the one before. It's easy to believe that we'd be good at dealing with change, since it's such an unconditional aspect of life … but nothing seems to be further from reality. For some reason, many people have difficulty in accepting change. Accepting change means accepting and submitting to the unknown, and that can be pretty scary. From a place of fear, even if this fear only is experienced subconsciously, resistance is evident. It feels uncomfortable and is often perceived as threatening.

Fear of the unknown

Resistance arises when change is experienced as a threat to three basic needs:

- autonomy (inability to influence the situation),
- relationship (a lack of connection with or desire to change),

- competence (a sense of being less competent in the new situation, perhaps through the perceived absence of skills).

Yet changes that seem to naturally take place, without being consciously noticed, are seldom met with much fear or resistance.

The Mission Possible-program aims to meet the three basic needs of the client in his process toward change to help him meet the necessary changes without fear. The preferred future is at the focal point of these three basic needs. Each and every small, positive change is observed, registered, recognized, and appreciated. Otherwise they might be missed or taken for granted and would lose their value in the process. For this reason, it is valuable for the client to keep a diary, logbook, or blog in which such details are recorded.

Recording and recognizing

A diary, in whatever form, provides a clear picture (as complete as possible) of all the major and minor positive changes that take place. The requirement of maintaining a diary ensures an ongoing alertness in recognizing new developments. This conscious, constant focus also ensures that even the smallest successes on the way toward the goal are seen and registered. Once seen and recorded, such seemingly minor steps can subsequently be employed with awareness and optimum effectiveness. They form the foundation for motivation that is maintained at an efficient level as well as promoting self-confidence. Such recognized and recorded successful developments are the fuel that maintains the momentum of the Mission Possible process.

Evaluation

There's a further advantage to this continuous monitoring: interim evaluations! Evaluating serves to strengthen the awareness that positive steps (the prime focus) *are* being taken. Even small signs of positive change are included and contribute toward the client's feeling good about his progress. Such an evaluation moment provides both coach and client with the excellent opportunity of looking forwards and backwards in the process. Looking back together at the previous session helps to structure new agreements concerning actions that your client still has to carry out, as well as providing a useful overview of the whole process.

Hidden benefits

Such an evaluation and overview help to distinguish positive, unanticipated additional benefits, developments that are not directly related to the clearly described end result and yet are valuable in the client's progress. It's correct to conclude that working on positive change often results in additional and unforeseen benefits.

Self-reflection

Maintaining a diary, blog, or other form of logbook has an extra effect on young people, who tend to be very much focused on the outside world – it serves as an invitation to self-reflection, turning their focus from the outside to the inside.

A case study from school

A young client sets himself the goal of taking more responsibility for his school achievements by spending more time on his schoolwork. While working on this task, all sorts of things happen, some expected, some unexpected; all in all, they can be considered extremely agreeable and welcome.

For example, for quite some time now, he's had no arguments with his parents about his earlier, poor academic achievements. The teachers also express themselves more positively about their student – they see that he is genuinely trying to do his best. The teachers have even offered to give him extra support to help him catch up on what he's missed out on.

His marks are getting better all the time. He's also become aware of the fact that, by keeping up with his homework, he's gradually spending less time each day on this work now that he's caught up with the lessons. Result? Some evenings he has a little more time to spend with his friends, and his parents have become more flexible if he wants to go out on the weekend.

Furthermore, even though he is somewhat reluctant to admit it, he feels more at home in the class. It's even got easier for him to get up in the morning now that he knows his homework is done and that he's familiar with the lesson material. All in all, going to school has become more attractive than he had previously thought possible.

In his blog, he writes regularly about these sorts of small observations, yet it is only later that he actually becomes aware of the implications when he reads and evaluates the blog together with his coach. He often laughs aloud at the fact that he noted such details but only now sees how valuable they are. As his program progresses and he approaches his target, writing his blog becomes a much more conscious process. Then it becomes increasingly clear that he is able to observe both large and anticipated positive developments as well as the positive, unexpected side effects.

Writing a diary, in whatever form suits the client, is an invitation to him to learn a number of important skills on his way to adulthood and autonomy, namely self-reflection and self-correction.

Fostering progress

It seems quite normal to be happy with indicators of positive progress that mark the way to the final goal. Yet it is precisely the *normalcy* that all too often blocks seeing all the positive developments. Besides, it's quite difficult for many people to acknowledge their own positive achievements and go as far as to even compliment themselves on them. All too often I hear "No big deal" or "Oh that ... yes, I hadn't really paid any attention to that." For many people, it's quite a challenge to be honest with themselves *and* to see others as they are. It's 'not done' to talk about personal achievements and successes; other people should not be put in the position of feeling jealous; it's 'not done' to be in any way better than others; and so on, and so on ... so many societal and cultural behavioral restrictions. Americans are well known for their enthusiasm: "Wow, fantastic! Awesome! That's incredible!"

Even during a first meeting, they have little hesitation in showcasing their personal successes, something that many from different cultures consider weird and exaggerated. But why shouldn't they openly express their pride in their achievements? What is wrong with recognizing personal success, so long as there's space to recognize and respect other people's achievements? There's room for everyone and every success! Everyone should be able to express himself freely: "I deserve to be here and take my place in the world!"

It should be possible to speak without restraint about positive progress and achievements – anything to support the sense of *having a right to exist*.

Fundamental right

The statement "I deserve to be here and take MY place in the world!" should not have to be *earned* – it's part of everyone's birthright but one that seems to have been forgotten by the time puberty sets in. Every positive development, even if it's just the expression of a clear goal, is worth recognizing. In this way, the sense of *having a right to be here and worthy* is reinforced.

Self-image

Fostering progress by recognizing that progress really is happening, *owning* it, and becoming aware of even the slightest improvements are powerful ways to enhance the self-image. A healthy self-image is required for young people to grow into successful and happy adults who live their lives fully.

Sharing with others

Your young client helps himself to experience all positive change as successes by keeping a diary – in whatever form – of all developments during his Mission Possible-program. Seeing positive developments helps him to stay motivated and supports working toward the final goal over a longer period of time. When he goes on to *share* his experiences with others, he also benefits from the positive responses from his supporters and even from those less directly involved. In turn, all such positive appreciation serves to further nourish his motivation.

Details

All experiences, even those the client judges to be less than good, can help him gain clarity about where he is on his way to the desired result and which steps he still has to take. If he records both what has taken place so far and what he has already achieved, there is less chance of missing important steps; even minor progress will then not so easily be overlooked.

Sharing

There's an added advantage: when he shares with, for example, his supporters, even if *he* has missed some detail, there's a good chance that someone else will pick up on it. Sharing information about his program and his progress is important both for the client *and* for his coach. This sharing is a valuable aid in evaluating and possibly revamping earlier agreements.

Tools

There are many advantages to monitoring and recording information about the client's progress through his Mission Possible-program and to *sharing* this easily. First and foremost, as already noted, there are the benefits to the coach–client partnership in reviewing activity. A useful tool is a large sheet of paper, like a flip chart, that visualizes the stages and progress and accompanies each session. This way, it gradually becomes an increasingly important work document (see the 'Tools for the toolbox' about the circle technique). Since most clients probably will prefer not to walk around with such a large piece of paper, it suffices to take a photo at the conclusion of each session. The client then has a personal, visual overview of his progress that he can use as reference material.

Keeping in touch

Furthermore, sharing positive information helps to keep both the client and his supporters closely involved in the process. These days, young people commonly use social media, so *that* is the most obvious choice as to how to share. However, not *everything* needs to be shared, and it's certainly unnecessary for your young client to be present in all his vulnerability on social media. Discussing what sort of information is suitable for posting should definitely be a point on the agenda. A restricted group app could provide the safest and wisest solution, but a different, nondigital form of sharing may be just as safe.

Selecting a form

How progress should be recorded is definitely a subject that deserves attention from the very start of the Mission Possible-program. As mentioned earlier, there are various options, each with its own pros and cons. Although of course it's ultimately the client who chooses how he will monitor and record his progress, as a coach, you are responsible for helping him make a conscious, well-balanced decision. Such a discussion and agreement lower the risk that your client unwittingly violates his own privacy ...

Social media

Although the current generation is growing up in the digital world of 'the internet of things', I never cease to be amazed at their open-mindedness and nonchalance in sharing sensitive, personal information on social media. That is why I am reluctant to endorse an open blog in which everything gets posted. Many young people blog. Social media form the global platform on which young people in every country keep in touch with each other and promote themselves and their activities. They share their own experiences, interests, and ideas with the world through fancy profile pages and channels on Facebook, Instagram, YouTube, Pinterest, TikTok, or whatever platform is currently fashionable. There are numerous examples of young people who have been extremely successful in showcasing their talents, attracting a large following and consequently even generating considerable income.

Privacy?

Because social media are an obvious place for a digital diary and young people feel comfortable in using them, it seems to be the right medium for them to record their progress and personal successes. But a serious warning should be given, considering that once information is posted on the internet, it's there for eternity and can be manipulated and passed on (into potentially wrong hands).

Traditional possibilities

Of course, it's fine if your young client prefers a different medium. A more traditional diary, a notebook, or some other creative work form can be equally effective. Most young people these days are not so fond of writing. They prefer to make videos, drawings, poems, collages, or whatever. The most important thing that matters is that, having chosen a suitable medium for expressing their feelings and experiences, there's also space for sharing with the coach and supporters.

Simplicity and effectiveness

What I've especially noticed in my own practice is that it is during the coaching sessions that agreements and progress are brought up to date, with client and coach working together. A large flip-chart sheet serves as a flexible and effective 'study document' during the whole program.

Tips and ideas for keeping log

It's important to discuss with your client the pros and cons:

- of the consequences of sharing information on the internet
- of the issues of privacy
- of having to deal with unwanted reactions from others (people outside his network)

Information, once posted, has a surprisingly long life. The same information has the habit of circulating through various channels, even if it's outdated, no longer relevant, and unwanted. In this way, posting personal information can have negative consequences in the long term. When you discuss all such matters in detail with your client, he will be able to make better and more conscious judgment about what he chooses to post.

Anonymity

One option is to use a Mission Possible code name to make the blog anonymous. By leaving out any personal details, your client can be more open in an anonymous blog about his ups and downs during the program. Moreover, his privacy will be protected for the future. Ask your client to select a code name that reflects his intended goal. The name of a person (a symbolic figure like Superman or Mickey Mouse), an animal, or symbol – there are many possibilities, so long as it is clear that it really is a *code* name. Just using the name of another, real-life person is naturally undesirable.

Content

Once your client has chosen a suitable, inspiring code name, you can go on to make agreements about what he may and may not write about. After all, there will certainly be information that should be kept just for a select group of friends and supporters that he can then share when there is personal contact. And, as mentioned earlier, apart from the blog, there is a whole range of media to support and visualize his progress: a (loose-leaf) notebook, flip-over sheets, posters (for on his bedroom wall), Post-its, collages of illustrations, words, and articles, letters, comics and cartoons that he draws himself, emails ... the list is endless and permits the client the space for his individual creativity and originality.

Chapter 6

Taking action

Now that the first steps on the way to your client's goal have been discussed, it's the right moment to give some attention to two important steps designed to maintain momentum in the program: managing setbacks and celebrating successes!

Since your young client is now involved in translating his goal or even multiple goals into concrete actions, it's vital to start taking these two issues into account and discussing them in detail with each other.

Step 10: Setbacks

Anyone who sets out to achieve a goal will sooner or later be confronted by the fact that the road is not always so smooth. There are stones, potholes, and even fallen trees to deal with, all of which can be hindrances on the way. This observation is so obvious that it's easy to ignore the reality of setbacks. It's a fact of life that, since the moment of birth, not everything goes precisely as is expected or preferred.

The value of setbacks

Daily setbacks and failures are just a normal part of life, even if experienced as less than agreeable. However, if you learn to accept such events as an inherent (and therefore normal) part of development, they can contribute positively to healthy self-esteem and self-confidence. These events are then valuable experiences (knowing what does *not* work!) as well as an equally valuable reminder that *everything* is temporary, that all things change and pass and get forgotten.

When your client has the right mindset focused on growth and development, setbacks cease to have any negative effect on the goal as it increasingly comes into sight. In other words, so long as setbacks can be reframed as 'learning experiences', then only benefits accrue.

That said, it is a fact that learning to reframe setbacks in this way is part of growing up, requiring a degree of emotional intelligence and maturity. Put another way, it's a skill that needs to be acquired.

Conditioning

From the outset of social programming, setbacks are mostly represented as threatening and negative. The need for a protection mechanism results in the development of a strategy for dealing with such threats, a strategy that prevents having to experience such an unpleasant 'surprise' again or at least softens the blow. A newly born baby experiences the harsh lighting of the delivery room as decidedly unpleasant after the soft, pinkish twilight of the womb. The hard sounds and firm handling, no longer dampened by the calming amniotic fluid, are equally harsh and painful. The birth process is, in most cases, a less than pleasant event.

Dependence

The baby soon learns that all beneficial and agreeable experiences come from outside, like being fed or having his diaper changed. He learns that he is dependent on others to have his needs met. And if Mum is otherwise occupied at the very moment that he demands attention, he feels disappointed and frustrated. The baby immediately feels that his survival is threatened and begins to cry. At that young time in his life, he has no other strategy available. That begins to change around the eighth month, when he starts experiencing the world from his own perspective, as his sense of a separate self ('I') begins to awaken.

Strategies

From that moment, the child realizes (unconsciously) that he can influence receiving those things that have an external source and starts developing a range of tricks to ensure his success.

"If I cry, Mum comes to change my diaper or feed me."
"If I laugh, I get lots of attention."

And so on. In this way, each child develops his own specific strategy, based on the impact of the initial trauma. These are lifetime strategies that remain active, although with plenty of possible variations on the basic theme. As the individual grows up, the strategies become less than productive and may even become counterproductive. But because such strategies have developed into purely automatic behavior, it is only with enormous effort that they can be transformed into more useful modes of behavior. Such a process of transformation requires time, awareness, and motivation.

Disappointment

When things go differently than hoped or expected, these are challenges that lead to disappointment and frustration. There's every chance of losing hope of achieving the preferred goal *and* of losing the motivation to continue. And such feelings – losing hope and motivation – are realistic precursors of depression. For young people, setbacks are all too often perceived as totally unexpected. After all, young people tend to live so intensely 'in the moment' that such setbacks are extremely nasty surprises that are hard to deal with. In fact, such unanticipated setbacks can have dramatic, even traumatic effects.

Example

Imagine an unexpected, dangerous moment, such as when a dog suddenly crosses the road in front of your bike or car. The shock can be enormous, and you feel the adrenaline boost in your body for quite some time, long after the dog has safely reached the other side of the road. Consider, however, the difference here: you're cycling in a park where dogs are allowed to run freely. You're *expecting* that a dog might cross your path, so you cycle more carefully, perhaps more slowly, and are more alert. If a dog does indeed get in your way, you're more prepared and can easily apply the brakes in time. Maybe there's still a degree of shock but with much less impact on the body; there's less adrenaline with its accompanying effects. Perhaps you express a sigh of relief that you managed to avoid the dog and were competent enough to respond in time. The situation is under control.

Trauma

In this last example, you are able to process the event rapidly. There is no sign of trauma. And *that* is the difference with unexpected situations, when it takes longer for the body to recover from the physical effects of the shock. *That* is the trauma – to the extent that the next time you get on your bike or in your car, the memory of the uncomfortable event returns. And even if you know it belongs in the past, your body responds with physical signals to that unprocessed memory. With any luck, you'll succeed in mastering your fear. In that event, you'll still be somewhat insecure about driving and unsure about whether you have everything under control.

Staying in charge

Adolescents have a strong tendency to want to be in charge of their lives. They have an equally strong urge toward independence, a clear characteristic of beginning adulthood. They are in a phase of life in which they are gradually becoming more aware of their need to pursue their own path.

Limiting beliefs

In adolescence, they have already had sufficient life experience to know that not everything they undertake immediately turns out well. This conditioning based on experience creates an unconscious belief system that plays a significant part in guiding their lives. Unconscious thought patterns lead to negative feelings, a reason such thoughts are called limiting beliefs. Put another way, the adolescent experiences the unconscious effect of these restrictive thoughts that lead to negative feelings and emotions. Altogether, these limiting beliefs and the physical reactions they stir obstruct the development of a positive mindset focused on growth and create stress when there's a setback.

Because this process takes place largely at an unconscious level during puberty, the limiting beliefs easily become part of the individual's identity; expressions such as these are then quite common:

"I can't do it. I'm not clever enough."
"I'm not going to even try that. Even if I do, there's no way it's going to work."

Ancient response mechanism

The basal ganglia or 'reptilian brain' is the oldest part of the brain. It is together with the limbic brain responsible for hormonal stress responses and, in adolescence, is working at perhaps its hardest. Fighting, fleeing, or freezing are useful and instantaneous responses that developed when man was wearing bearskins and had to deal with saber-toothed tigers and other aggressive animals and when split-second reactions determined who would be whose next meal!

Speed!

The reptilian brain, with its instinctive reactions, is much faster than the frontal cortex (the 'thinking brain') that developed later in man's evolution. In ancient times, responses were required much sooner than the frontal cortex, with all its deliberations, could provide. It's very likely that man would have soon become extinct *without* the reptilian brain!

The trap of 'explanations'

In adolescence, the combination of the responsive reptilian brain and the cognitive frontal cortex results in an additional complication. The instinctive response – fight, flee, or freeze – gets interpreted under the influence of all sorts of limiting beliefs. Such beliefs, already constructed by earlier positive and negative experiences, are then used to explain disappointments away. Below are some real-life examples from practice:

The futility of taking action

"I've already told you that I can never get things right. I'm jinxed." *(freeze)*
"Nobody's out there to help me." *(freeze)*
"I'm totally useless." *(freeze)*

Avoiding taking action

"I'm off." *(flee)*
"There's no point in my hanging around. I never get things right." *(flee)*

Confrontation

"If they touch me, I'll really get wild." *(fight)*
"If they want trouble, they can have it!" *(fight)*

Powerlessness

It is worth noting the connection between the freeze response and the role of victim that is taken on. This is then a situation dominated by the loss of independence and the feeling of being unable to exert any influence. Early experiences of stress, fear, and disappointment – when the child was too small to influence his surroundings – all too often lead to a sense of powerlessness. Such feelings are inevitably linked to one or more limiting beliefs, primarily at the level of identity, and expressed, for example, as "I'm stupid." Similar limiting beliefs are very much present in the minds of adolescents; they serve to undermine trust in their own basic needs and any hope of a positive result.

Reframing

The previous section makes it clear why it's better to recognize the presence of such mechanisms and to find ways of dealing with them constructively. The Solution Focused approach chooses *positive reframing* or *looking for exceptions*. As a coach, it's up to you to be persistent, as the following case example indicates:

Coach: Anil, I've just heard you say that you're always unlucky and that nothing succeeds straight away with you. May I go into this more deeply and ask some more questions?
Anil: Yes, okay, why?
Coach: Well, to go into the truth of why things never seem to work for you. What do you think?

Anil: Okay.

Coach: Looking back on your life, Anil, are there any moments when things actually went just right? It doesn't matter how long ago it was.

Anil: No idea. I'll have to think about that. Oh, wait a minute, though … When I was four years old, I nearly died. I'd drunk some cleaning fluid from the kitchen cabinet. My mum found me and called the ambulance immediately. That saved my life. My mum is my hero! So that was actually really bad luck that turned out okay in the end. I wouldn't be here otherwise.

Coach: My goodness, that's quite a story! And, Anil, what you describe is precisely what I'm talking about. Bad luck, and I mean when things go seriously wrong, can really get in your way. Then it's all too easy to forget that things *do* go well sometimes. It's not as if the same problem is a permanent feature in your life. And in your case, wow, it's indeed lucky that all turned out well. There must have been an angel watching over you.

Anil: Yes, my mum says that, too, sometimes, but then in my case, not so much an angel as a mischievous imp.

Coach: Now you're laughing! Great! Tell me, are there any other moments when you were successful even if it was difficult?

Anil: I recently had an argument with some boys about a sum of money that I had to pay back. I'd borrowed the money during the break to buy some cigarettes. But I didn't have it in time to pay them back. They got angry and wanted to start a fight. I was pretty scared, as there were three of them. But I stayed calm and explained that I just didn't have the money at that moment and that I'd be able to repay them two days later after I got the wages from my part-time job. They agreed, and we shook hands on the deal. And of course, I really did return what I owed them. And guess what? They actually said that it was cool what I did – after all, they'd wanted to fight, and I'd shown them another way to resolve the argument. But I'm not going to borrow any more money, even if I don't have anything to smoke.

Coach: How would you describe this experience now, Anil? Was this bad luck, a failure, or something else?

Anil: Well, in the beginning, it wasn't any fun, because I didn't have any money at that moment. That's just bad luck. And it was my bad luck that these guys got angry. But in the end, it wasn't that bad at all, and certainly not a failure, because I managed to find a solution.

Coach: So, how would you describe what happened?

Anil: Well, actually, I was pretty lucky and everything turned out okay.

Coach: Is there anything else you could learn from this? Like, what did you actually do that created the solution?

Anil: Oh, nothing special. I thought about it, didn't pee in my pants *[broad grin]*, and came up with something that would be okay with them. Oh yes, and of course I've learned that borrowing money isn't such a good idea – after all, the money still has to be repaid.

Coach: Wonderful! I have nothing to add ... except, what were you saying earlier about always having bad luck and that you never succeeded at anything?

[Laughter]

Preparing for obstacles

An effective way of being prepared for possible setbacks is to recognize them and to discuss them *before* they might happen. It is much easier to deal with setbacks once it can be accepted that they are a normal and inevitable part of life. Including setbacks as a normal part of any process is an excellent way of counteracting any potentially damaging effects like disappointment, frustration, and loss of motivation. As a well-known management guru once said, "Shit happens."

Be prepared

It is better to be realistically aware in advance of this simple fact and to then take any necessary steps. Result? The surprise is reduced to a minimum so that in the end, it's no longer a shock when something goes wrong. The negative impact is significantly less. It's easier to look at what happens objectively, thereby taking it less personally. The simple awareness that setbacks are a natural and normal part of everybody's life makes them easier to accept. Although it's still necessary to accept responsibility, there is no longer an automatic sense of guilt and shame.

It's definitely beneficial to be well prepared, much better than:

- *fight*: trying to maintain a positive attitude while, deep inside, being aware of a different reality
- *flight/freeze*: losing motivation and giving up.

Preparation includes mental as well as practical aspects and therefore both cognitive as well as behavioral approaches to possible obstacles.

Helping change to happen

When letting go of old patterns of thought and behavior, the same natural laws appear to apply as with different, more material processes. Where something is – as it were – removed, a gap or vacuum is created, and this gap or vacuum *will* naturally get filled. This will either be by something that has consciously been chosen or by something that has not been chosen and may be undesirable. Take the familiar story of the smoker who at last stops smoking but has to go on a diet to curb his excessive eating.

'Old habits die hard'

Falling back onto old habits is, alas, all too easy. The brain is wired in such a way that it prefers taking the easiest route, which usually means an old, existing route. Comparison: it takes much more energy (and money) to make a new motorway through a jungle than to add an extra lane to an existing highway.

Dealing with setbacks and relapses

"What is the best way of dealing with possible setbacks?"

This is a realistic question that your young client should first try to answer for himself. After all, it's about finding solutions that suit *him*. But the answers to this crucial question are surprisingly simple. He is already familiar with the idea of accepting obstacles and setbacks as a normal part of the learning process. Also that it's all right to learn through trial and error. However, there *are* additional valuable options.

Simple solutions

First and foremost, it's worthwhile thinking about concrete steps that can be taken to deal with possibly disagreeable situations *before* they happen. Get your young client to come up with plans for how he would like to deal with setbacks long before he actively starts working toward his goal. When he's got a number of clear steps lined up 'in case of emergency,' he's going to lower the chance of panicking when something unexpected starts to happen. The only aspect that is then unexpected is the precise moment when it happens! He can then act on a choice of the options that he'd thought of and discussed with you earlier in his process.

"Help!"

One of the steps he can take is to agree on a signal (verbal or nonverbal) that he can give to his friends and supporters. They in turn then know that your client has temporarily lost sight of his goal and needs some support and reminders or that he's experiencing a setback. Part of the 'emergency plan' is to ask a specific supporter to function as a help desk, to whom he can turn for support when things seem to be going wrong. Each and every plan that the client thinks of is welcome. The more useful plans your client can come up with, the better.

Ultimately, it's great to choose a plan that best suits the specific, current situation. And in a situation when, for example, the help desk supporter is unavailable as first choice of action, there should be other viable options that have already been considered.

Case in question

A girl was using her Mission Possible-program to complete her education successfully. She experienced difficulty in working toward her goal but thought up seven different plans to support herself for when things would go wrong. And just in case even those seven plans were inadequate, she'd thought up an eighth plan:

> "I'm going to bake myself a cake – just for me!"
> When asked about the background to this creative plan, she replied:

> > "If nothing seems to be working right, then it's time to comfort myself, because I have been doing my best. I then appreciate myself for all the effort I've put into the program so far. I love baking cakes – I always feel happy when baking! So at such a moment, I'm going to choose to do something that shifts my mood, that makes me happy. When I'm happy and back in the mood, I'll automatically have the energy to move on again."

Such wisdom and self-love! Her answer indicates that truly *anything* and everything can potentially be of use, as long as it is the client who determines it to be a good solution to overcoming a setback.

Helpful questions

There are many questions that you could ask to help your client find the best solutions for dealing with setbacks, such as these:

> "Imagine you get into a situation in which you temporarily lose sight of your goal or forget to learn your new skill. How would you then like to be reminded to start working again?"
> "What do you think you'd need in order to get moving again on your program?"
> "Who or what could help you then?"
> "What has worked before to help keep you motivated?"
> "What have you done in the past to keep going when you were working toward a goal? How would *that* help you now, with this program?"

There are, of course, many more questions than just these. Depending on each individual situation, numerous different questions would be suitable. In the end, it's all up to you, your creativity, and your flexibility to help your client find the answers himself.

Link to real life

You've now reached the point at which you support your young client in applying all that he's learned in everyday, practical life.

What tools does he have at his disposal, and how can he best apply them?

Together you can, for instance, make a *risk analysis*:

"What do you think could possibly go wrong on your way to your goal?"

It's possible that your client experiences a temporary lack of drive and motivation, perhaps through some external factor. It's equally possible that during a certain period, little or no significant progress is made. In this latter event, the absence of positive developments can act as a brake on the motivation to keep going on the path to the preferred goal.

Reevaluating the goal?

There are many possible reasons setbacks occur. However, analysis indicates that a number of well-designed questions can help to restore momentum. As a coach, you might wonder whether it's useful to evaluate the current goal and perhaps to adjust it in some way. It should be noted that one of the best-known pitfalls is selecting a goal that is too abstract or simply too large. Looking closely at the goal and adjusting it is an excellent option that helps get the young client moving to progress again.

Three (groups of) questions to resolve stagnation

"Are you absolutely sure that the goal you've chosen still is the one you want to work on? Or is there perhaps something that is actually more important to you?"

While working toward a specific goal, it occasionally happens that the coach and/or the client discover that a different goal would be more in alignment with what the client needs and wants at that particular moment. As the program progresses, it does become clearer what the client genuinely wants. In that case, it is better to redefine or refine the goal instead of simply continuing on the existing path. Using the peel protocol (as described in Step 1) is a sensible way to minimize the risk of this pitfall.

"How do you do those things that really work well for you? How do you take the right steps that help you to get closer to your goal?"

If the selected goal is truly the *right* one, but there are simply too few positive indications of growth toward it, then it is certainly correct to ask if the *right* steps have been taken:

"The steps that you've taken, have they had any effect? Have they worked? Or would it be better if you did something different?"

This is an area in which supporters could almost certainly help your client to gain the necessary clarity. Perhaps they have useful ideas for steps that might be more effective. It may well be possible to distinguish valuable actions that genuinely worked in the steps that have been taken. However, these actions may prove to be much more effective when applied in a different way at a different moment.

"What more is needed? Is anything different needed?"

Imagine that the chosen goal is the right one; imagine that solid steps have been taken and progress has been made toward the goal; is it then possible that important external resources are missing? Are more supporters required? Or is more information, coaching, or time required? Would expanding self-confidence help? Or would simply more patience and time be sufficient to get the job done?

Even if not everything is going so smoothly, in the vast majority of cases, it will still be possible to observe positive developments. However, it does occasionally happen that the desire to achieve the goal is so strong that impatience restricts a clear view of the progress made. This observation serves to confirm the importance of continual monitoring of progress during the program and the associated value of a logbook or diary. It is only in this way that even the smallest positive change can be discerned and, most importantly, never missed.

A case study from practice: Joan

Coach: Hello, Joan, good to see you again. How have things been going for you in the last week?

Joan: Hello, Coach. It's good to be back here again with you. Y'know, it was all a bit confusing. I first thought there was no point in coming to see you – nothing seems to be happening. That didn't feel right either, but when I started making my vlog [video blog] – well, I'd been out with some friends first – when I started, then I also started seeing it differently.

Coach: How interesting! Want to tell me more?

Joan: Sure … that's when I realized I'd been getting all worked up for nothing. Not for myself, but because I didn't want to waste your time. Well … and that's when I thought I'd let you down.

Coach: Oh?

Joan: When I was making the video clip, I was really honest, y'know. I said that I felt I hadn't done enough this week, and that I regretted that, too. But a girlfriend who was helping me with my video said that she thought it was really cool what I said, that I'd honestly thought it all over and so on. Yes, also that I said that I felt I'd let you down. And then I thought, wow, that's quite an important change – y'know, mostly I don't give a shit what other people think about me or about what I do. And y'know what, I've noticed that *that* just isn't true! I was just fooling myself all the time. I really *DO* care what others think and also whether my behavior irritates them.

Coach: Wow, Joan, I'm impressed! Yes, I fully agree with you. What you've discovered is a very important change – or actually, it's more of an insight. Would you like to tell me how you came to realize this about yourself?

Joan: I don't actually know. I felt really uncomfortable about it all. I couldn't stop thinking about it all, and I felt guilty – yes, the whole week. All the time! I thought it was really weird, y'know, that I felt this way and still didn't do anything that we'd agreed upon.

Coach: It's true, Joan, that you haven't exactly done what we agreed on together. But as I listen to you, I get the feeling that you've done something really important this week, something that's perhaps even more important than what was planned. You should know that I'm very happy with what you've shared with me. Joan, why do you think I'm happy with you?

Joan: Hmm ... well, perhaps it's because this week, I've really been thinking over how I come across, what I'm like, and what I've always done, and so on. And what that means to other people. That's why I felt guilty. But of course, that doesn't help much – I have to do something about it.

Coach: *[At first, silent]* I hardly know what to say, Joan – I'm impressed by what you're telling me. You've noticed that you feel uncomfortable and guilty about not having kept our agreement. And you've also noticed that feeling like this doesn't help you to move on and get things done. You discovered that something else – like action on your part – is required to get everything moving smoothly. I think that this is true for others, too, not only for you. What do *you* think?

Joan: Yes, I can see how it all fits together now and that it's up to me to do something. Also, that it doesn't help just to sit around feeling lousy. And I *was* feeling rotten even though I didn't say anything about it. And by bottling it all up, I only got angrier with everyone around me. I feel pretty bad about that now.

Coach: I hear you say that you feel pretty bad about that now. How does it help you to feel sorry about how you behaved?

Joan: Hmm ... not sure ... perhaps it *does* help a bit. Yes and no. In any case, it *does* help to look at things differently. I really would like things to be different.

Coach: That seems like quite a discovery, Joan! I think you've used your time well this week, thinking over things so well. That is in itself a step in the right direction, and it's definitely produced results! Especially since your honesty has clarified matters for you so well. What do *you* think?

Joan: Yes, that's true. I hadn't seen it quite like that before.

Coach: Joan, our time together today is nearly up. Is there anything else you'd like to tell me or ask before we discuss our next meeting?

Joan: No idea right now, Coach. We've talked about far more things than I had previously thought about. Actually, I was rather concerned that you might be p****d off with me because I hadn't kept our agreements.

Coach: Of course I like it when you keep your agreements with me, and you truly have kept a number of them. Which ones can you think of?

Joan: What do you mean? That I've done what I agreed to do?

Coach: Yes.

Joan: Oh ... now I need to think about what we'd actually agreed on. Uh ... That I'd come here today? And that I'd talk to my mentor about the situation in the class and what I could do about it myself. Oh yes, and that I'd update my vlog, because I'd forgotten to do that the time before. And that I'd think about what I could do to behave in a friendlier way. But we'd only talked about my *thinking* about all this, not that I had to do it all immediately.

Coach: Correct! Nothing wrong with your memory! Can you be more precise about which of the agreements you haven't done anything about?

Joan: Oh ... that I'd talk with my mentor. I didn't get around to that.

Coach: Exactly. Joan, that's the only one ... but besides that, you've done a lot more than what we agreed on last time. You've thought about a number of the issues and also started doing something about them. I'm very pleased – it's much more than I'd expected or hoped for. What do you think we can agree on for next week?

Joan: [*big smile*] Oh, that's easy, and I really will. Promise! I can see now that it's much better for me when I share with others what I'm going through. It's weird that something which I used to see as wrong or stupid has actually helped me.

Coach: I understand. Sometimes we just look the wrong way and miss what's actually happening. Okay, off you go; it's time to stop. I look forward to seeing you next week. I'm enjoying working with you, Joan! Good luck! Oh yes, may I take a look at your vlog?

Joan: [*Laughter*] Of course you can. That's what it's there for ... right?

Coach: What do *you* think?

Joan: [*big smile, with the doorknob in her hand*] Okay! I'll think about that too this week. Bye!

Step 11: Celebrating success

There comes a moment when your client has reached enough positive developments that it would be correct to talk about his success. True, the definition of 'success' and when it's time to label progress toward the goal as success remains subjective. It depends on each individual's own perception. It goes without saying that your personal projections as a coach must be excluded as much as possible from the client's process. In Solution Focused coaching, 'success' is certainly not clearly defined. The perspective of the young client, together with the agreements he made with his coach, ultimately determines the success of a Mission Possible-program.

When to celebrate success?

It's time to celebrate when the goal, the desired or preferred future, is in sight or when it's time to evaluate important progress made toward the goal. Then it's the right moment to pay full attention to all positive changes that have taken place and to appreciate and celebrate the serious efforts taken. Such a moment is also the perfect occasion for letting the supporters share in the glow of success as well as to thank them for their contribution.

Sharing success

This is an excellent moment to ask your client whom he would like to share his success with:

> "Who do you wish to tell about your milestone? With whom would you like to share your success?"

In many situations, it can be extremely valuable to share information about successful developments, for example, what goal your client has set for himself and what positive change he has genuinely achieved. Sharing what the client has learned and the positive changes that he underwent with significant others in his network provides the network with useful information. *This* helps them to better recognize and appreciate any changes. In this way, the client influences and restores his relationship with his network with new positive experiences, making them an important resource for support. The existence of such a supportive network encourages him in maintaining his growth-mindset to continue working on creating positive changes.

Evaluation

An evaluation meeting at the end of the Mission Possible-program enables you both to look back at how things went. Together, you can look in detail at the important points that contributed to this achievement. Under your guidance, the client checks whether he has met all previously made agreements and has taken all the required steps. Together, you decide if the initially described future, the goal, is reached or at least has been brought much closer. And if this is the case, then it's the right moment to celebrate the client's success! This evaluation moment becomes much easier when, at the start of the Mission Possible-program, the criteria for success as well as when it's time to celebrate are discussed and recorded in detail.

Overcoming the inner critic

In general, young people are extremely critical about their achievements. All too often, they underestimate or even downsize their efforts and progress. Moreover, they tend to ignore or deny the importance of recognizing and appreciating their own successes, even when the goal is in plain sight.

It is precisely here that you play an important part in helping your client to genuinely recognize and appreciate his achievements. When you ask questions that help your client become more aware of his efforts and the many inner resources he put to use, and you give compliments, directly or indirectly, you help him to 'own' his success. Below are some questions that may help in promoting the client's awareness of his skills:

"Many people set goals but give up on the way. Have you any idea what it was that enabled you to be so persistent?"
"Will you tell me how you managed that?"
"Which steps have you taken to bring your goal closer?"
"How did you know what was the right thing to do?"
"What was helpful for you?"
"Who was able to support you?"
"How did you manage to stay motivated, even when you were experiencing setbacks?"

Compliments

It is more or less self-evident that you pay one or more compliments to the client after he answers such questions. In practice, it turns out that after such an exchange, it's much easier for the client to receive and accept a compliment. After becoming aware of and acknowledging his resources and efforts, it's as if a sense of *mastery* starts to appear; false modesty is then gradually replaced by genuine pride in his own achievements.

When is the time to talk about success?

What one person considers a success may not be much reason for celebration for somebody else. For young people, too, success is subjective. Each individual will have his own definition of what a successful program constitutes. From the very start, therefore, it is important to make clear agreements about what your client's success at the end of the program looks like.

The clearer and more specific the description of the goal is, the easier it will be to determine whether that result has truly been achieved. Being specific about both the preferred actions and skills *and* the time in which this result should be achieved means little uncertainty can arise about what could be described as successful. From start to finish of the program, the client knows what is expected of him. There can't be any confusion for the client about when the goal should be reached and what it looks like.

Clear structure, easy monitoring

Such a degree of clarity provides a solid framework, a supportive structure during the client's process. At an early stage, you and the client can plan when interim evaluation moments would be useful, just like taking that opportunity to peel the goal in smaller subgoals. This makes it easier for both parties to monitor progress effectively. With a clear structure, it's easy for your client to answer the following questions at virtually any moment during the program:

"Are you on track?" or "Have you reached the goal when you wanted to, hoped to, and agreed to?"

As soon as this last question can be answered with a resounding 'yes' or 'almost,' it is time to discuss the subject of celebrating success once again.

Trust in a positive outcome

It is advisable to discuss these topics together at the start of the process so that the possibility of a successful achievement of the preferred goals only can be experienced as the inevitable outcome. By discussing the details of celebrating success at the start of the program, you implicitly give your young client the message that there is great confidence in the good outcome.

Different ways of defining success

It's not obvious that you and the client always will define success as reaching the preferred goal at the end of the program. It can be perfectly fine to regard a final evaluation as marking a time path that was mapped out at the start of the program. The end situation can also be marked with a scaling exercise, which can be used at several moments during the Mission Possible process to monitor progress. You and your client can agree that it doesn't have to be a perfect 10.

Equally well, when setting goals, the client doesn't necessarily have to aim at the ideal situation. This 'perfect 10' on the scale can also serve as a reason for stress, and it seems then quite meaningless to strive for perfection just for the sake of being perfect. Striving for personal excellence, your client becoming the best he can be, can be enough to be satisfied and able to look back at a successfully completed program.

A case study from practice: Kevin

Coach: Kevin, now the moment has come for you. You've been working so hard and have now reached your goal! You wanted to learn to be more considerate of others instead of frequently ending up in conflicts. Now it seems that you have achieved that quite nicely, your supervisor tells me. Tell me, what do *you* think?

Kevin: Yes, that's right, I really think so too! *[He smiles broadly]* Yes, I feel really proud of myself. And so does my Gran, you know. Now that I have a job and have stopped hanging out on the streets, everything is different. People are so much nicer to me. I no longer get so upset by them. You know, it's really great to see how glad my Gran is when she sees me walking up past her window. Then she's glowing all over. I was really touched when she even burst out in tears one time. And she gave me such a loving hug. So sweet, that old woman ... *[Smiles again]* And before, she used to just complain to me ...

Coach: That all sounds really great, Kevin. So, would you agree that it's time to celebrate your success?

Kevin: Wow, yes, I guess so ... I haven't actually made it to 10. But sure, it's a steady 9 now. I'm satisfied if it stays like this.

Coach: Sure! You have every right to be very proud, Kevin. Truly, you've achieved a lot. Now, what would you like to do to celebrate?

Kevin: My boss has said I can use the canteen at work. He told me that after he'd spoken to you. I think that would be cool. There's a bar and a sound system. But I want to keep it fairly quiet. I just want it to be chill, because my Gran must be able to come too! You know what? She says she'd like to meet my friends. She says that if they've supported me that much, they must be pretty okay guys. And when she said that, I got a lump in my throat. It *is* true – even if there are people out there who think differently – these friends really helped me enormously, through a lot of shit. Oops, I mean bad times. I owe them because *they* helped me get here now, and of course, my Gran. She always believed in me. She's always stood by me.

Coach: Right, Kevin – and don't forget your own efforts. You've really worked hard to get it done. And truly, I know it's not always been easy for you. You've achieved much more than just getting yourself off the streets. You've accepted all offers of help, you've listened closely to what was offered, and at the same time, you've cut down your smoking pot. Especially with the latter, you've managed to get more clarity about what you really want to do and what is truly important for you.

I want you to know how very proud I am of you and that I'd love to come to your party. Isn't it great that your boss is so understanding and is willing to let you use his facilities? This shows that he really believes in you, Kevin. I wouldn't want to miss this party for the world! You will let me know if I can help in any way with the organization?

Kevin: Sure, Coach – thanks!

The value of celebrating success

This last step in the Mission Possible-program is often underrated. False modesty, perhaps, shyness about being at the center of attention, or limiting beliefs are all possible reasons to block serious recognition of one's own success. All too often, it's viewed as something obvious or 'normal' ("No big deal") and something unworthy of being emphasized. And of course, there's always the risk of being criticized ("Show-off!"). The general norm seems to be to not stand out from the crowd.

Success is a team effort

Although a degree of modesty is definitely valued, when it comes to celebrating success in the context of Mission Possible, there's much more involved than just getting applause and taking the winner's place on the stage. Successful outcomes rarely come from the efforts of just one person. Of course, the winner of the gold medal for the 1000 meters personally ran that distance in the fastest time. But there's a whole team behind him, making it possible for him to perform at this level: the supporters who encourage him, the logistics crew that makes all the travel arrangements, the coach, the loving friends and family members – altogether, they create the right setting in which the champion could win his medal.

It's a team effort! For this reason, celebrating reaching the goal is much more than praising the champion for his achievement. This is a sincere moment to recognize that 'no man is an island' and that others are required for optimum results. Everyone involved has played their part and worked together toward the result: a gold medal. Everyone was necessary in the process. Perhaps the true value of celebrating success is the recognition and validation of this cooperative process. Each contributor has a reason to be proud, to appreciate *and* to feel appreciated. Naturally, the first place goes to the champion himself, to your young client who has reached his goal ... but in the end, it's all about the group as a whole that contributed to the achievement.

Social network

Apart from purely personal aspects, an important value of the successful accomplishment of the Mission Possible-program is strengthening bonds, restoring or strengthening damaged relationships, and/or establishing a new, broader social network. There's more than enough scientific research available to confirm the importance of being part of a strong social network, with its benefits of a longer, happier, and healthier life.

Celebrating is valuable!

There's a huge amount of evidence-based information that confirms the advantages of celebrating success together. For everyone involved, to feel genuinely satisfied with and proud of a job well done is of considerable importance. It's a milestone for the client's self-confidence as well as for his entire community. Each success paves the way for the next. And

Tools for the toolbox

Take time to review the whole Mission Possible-program with your client. Refer as much as possible to the diary (notes, circle, logbook, vlog ...). Take some time looking at all the developments he's gone through. Together, you can make a list of the distinguishable positive changes. And you can ask your client to mark his highlights during the program.

Guidelines for the conversation:

- Discuss what you have both observed.
- Talk about changes that have truly contributed to successfully finishing the program.
- Identify specific actions that served to bring the goal closer.
- Ask your client what aspect or event he is most proud of.
- Think of what other people, supporters as well as others involved, have been most outspoken about in their praise.

It goes without saying that this is *not* the right time for modesty, true or false! As coach, feel free to expand on and appreciate everything that went well. True, many adolescents (and many adults too!) are hesitant to express pride in their achievements and to acknowledge their own positive contribution in their success. You might want to provide some extra encouragement here.

success can then be achieved more easily *and* with more confidence in a positive outcome.

Investment in the future

As a coach, you have the important task of helping your client become increasingly satisfied, proud, and self-confident. And it is equally important to help him to *allow and accept* these feelings without the interference of his limiting beliefs and to learn simply to enjoy and share them. It's a benefit that appreciation for the things that helped and worked make inner resources accessible for the client. In this way, all his experience as well as the required skills and qualities become available, to be fruitfully employed on a next occasion. All in all, awareness of these newly acquired resources improve your client's sense of competence to deal with future challenges and achieve new goals.

To sum up, here is a list of the various reasons for and benefits of celebrating success:

- It's a reward for a 'job well done'.
- It marks the end of the Mission Possible-program.
- It signals a fresh start, a new beginning.
- All supporters and others who were involved get to be appreciated and thanked for their contribution.
- It strengthens social bonds.
- It assures the client of support and encouragement when another occasion arises.
- It raises self-confidence.
- It generates or reawakens the trust of supporters and his immediate social context.
- It helps the client to become aware of his inner resources, such as skills, qualities, and the value of his experiences.
- It is an excellent opportunity to share the news of his success.
- It is an opportunity to celebrate and have some fun!

Perfect occasion

If your client wants to celebrate his success together with his supporters, it's a perfect occasion for outlining new steps for the future. Whether he makes a new promise or sets a new goal, it's a beautiful moment for healing old wounds. When everybody's in a festive mood, it's so much easier for him to apologize for his unwelcome behavior in the past.

Thanking supporters, acknowledging their contribution

Of course, it's wonderful for your client to feel satisfied about what he's achieved, and the satisfaction is even greater when he's able to share it. When he acknowledges and specifies the positive contribution of his supporters in his success, he's ensuring himself of their continued support in the future.

Building strong and lasting connections

It is as important for adolescents as it is for adults to have a strong, broad-based social network. These days, most young people seem to be well aware of this. Often, their peer network is strong and active, but their network sometimes lacks social contacts outside this peer group. As a Mission Possible coach, you can encourage your young client to invite supporters from farther afield than just his direct circle of friends. When you enlarge the diversity within the network of supporters, the variety of support expands. It's a bit similar to 'sometimes needing a carpenter, and on another occasion needing a plumber.' You'd want the best fitting support for each job. And when every supporter gets to do the job he's best at, thanking them for their contribution will be a valuable experience for all. It's a great way to restore and strengthen damaged or weak bonds.

Acknowledgment

Your young client reaches an important milestone when he is able to recognize and accept that the encouragement and contribution provided by his supporters represent a significant part of his achievement. All the more reason for him to pay attention to the role of his supporters during the celebration:

- looking back over the project;
- describing the successful cooperation;
- reviewing all that has taken place and has been achieved;
- emphasizing how the steps were taken with the supporters' help and input.

This is, all in all, a powerful moment to express solidarity. It is also a moment for each participant in the program – client, supporters, friends – to feel proud of himself, the other contributors, the family-and-friends network, and of course the client. It is such a powerful, shared moment as this that nourishes an optimistic approach to the future.

Celebration: added value

It's up to your client to choose any sort of celebration or party that he considers suitable. A prime condition is that it should be possible for all supporters to attend and that they can feel comfortable with the chosen form. After all, it's the occasion when the client's process and goal are to be evaluated! A central ingredient of the festive get-together is to discuss the various steps taken, the numerous activities and their effect, and, above all, each individual's contribution. It is valuable for all that it's more than just informative to hear what has actually contributed to the client's success. Many of them will, even if unintended, learn a thing or two from the experience. And what has worked now may work well again next time. This way, everyone learns not just about their mistakes and setbacks but especially about their potential, too.

Chapter 7

Tricks of the coaching trade

Solution Focused coaching seems quite simple, and in essence, it *is*. The power of the approach resides in its simplicity. The underlying vision and theory are relatively straightforward and easy to understand. However, it is an approach that requires a different perspective, a paradigm shift, in order to apply the concept in the best and most effective way. Even if you are able to make this switch with any degree of ease, it could very well be that your personal conditioning restricts how effectively you are able to adapt.

The pitfalls

It takes a lot of practice and, above all, awareness of personal patterns of thinking and conditioning in order to implement the principles of Solution Focused coaching with optimal effectiveness. You must first experience the pitfalls that lie in wait for you as a coach. Then, as you become aware of them, you will start learning to avoid them – alas, a process that demands considerable patience and perseverance to keep learning. Luckily, the Solution Focused approach is exceptionally forgiving and flexible. You can always reformulate your question and repeat a step or even cancel it as you move on. The key is to be aware of the fact that there *are* pitfalls. Then you learn to recognize them and go on to set everything straight again.

Authenticity

There's seldom much involved in correcting your course: it suffices to acknowledge aloud that you've gone off course and introduce a new intervention. Whether you ask a new, better-formulated question or go back to a moment before your error, it doesn't matter – the Solution Focused approach and its basic principles supply you with all the tools you need. Communicating transparently and authentically means you don't have to hide or pretend anything. It's allowed to state that you don't know, that you've asked the wrong question, or whatever. Showing that you are normal, human, and fallible underlines the equality of your position in relation to your client

and offers many opportunities for growth in the coach–client partnership –
growth for both parties involved.

Sorts of pitfall

There are four different categories of potential pitfalls while working with
the Solution Focused approach, each category with its own root cause.

Category 1

You return unconsciously to the problem. Often your client may precipitate
this, perhaps because he is still used to the conventional style of focusing
on problems while working with regular social workers or medical doctors.
Or he might simply need a little more validation of his feelings around the
problem.

Category 2

You get into trouble because of your unconscious or careless use of language, or you forget to reframe your client's negatives into positives.

Category 3

You get entangled in your own judgments and beliefs and, for a while, lose
sight of your client's worldview. When you are confronted with your client's case file, it's sometimes hard to ignore the history and your personal
objectives.

Category 4

Last, but by no means unimportant, there's the series of pitfalls you can land
in when you're working with clients that are not motivated yet to change
in the formal sense of the Mission Possible-program and are maybe not yet
ready for this step in their development. Similarly, and in this same category,
there's the pitfall of being carried away by your own enthusiasm and asking
your client to take steps in his development that are too large for him or that
he is not completely ready for.

Overlap

Naturally, there is some overlap within and between these four categories,
especially concerning pitfalls with more than one root cause. Experience
proves that sooner or later, more or less every Solution Focused coach will
come across them all. And some pitfalls you'll land in more than once. But

for every pitfall, there's a serious consolation: getting out of them is easy to do. As soon as you become aware of the wrong path that you took, you can flexibly and creatively deal with the situation and turn things for the better. There's no shame in just naming what doesn't work in that moment and asking your client for his permission to leave there and try something else instead. Using the key principles of the Solution Focused approach to get back on course to 'what works' gives you all opportunity to be totally transparent.

An overview of the most common pitfalls:

Category 1: focus on problems

- talking about the problem more than needed
- finding the cause or source of the problem (analyzing)
- blaming something or someone
- focusing on faults and deficits (whatever does *not* work)
- using accusing explanations

Category 2: language

- bad translation (from problem to preferred future)
- using complex language
- hopeless explanation (without any hope for improvement)
- personal interpretations of words and idioms
- using problem-focused language

Category 3: prejudice

- expecting resistance
- applying ill-fitting theory
- too much knowledge (preinformation)
- working solution forced instead of Solution Focused
- thinking the client needs helping or 'rescuing'

Category 4: no basis for motivation

- not having a 'customer' for change (not yet a commitment)
- trying to resolve an insoluble problem
- placing the client 'inside' the problem
- taking steps that are too large (going too fast)

Climbing out

The previous chapter described how relatively easy it is to recognize when you've landed in a pitfall: the flow of the conversation becomes somewhat awkward, and cooperation stagnates, you lose your client's rapport, and so on. In one way or another, rapport – the 'click' between you and your client – wanes. These are just some signs indicating that there's something wrong. This can be an uncomfortable moment for the inexperienced Mission Possible coach, but in fact, there's little to get anxious about. It's virtually impossible to avoid such pitfalls at all times, which is a good reason to simply accept that they're a normal part of the learning process. What *is* important is to stay calm and start looking for a way out – which may be surprisingly easy.

Take a break and rewind

Even if it only lasts a few seconds, breathe out and enjoy the silence as you silently evaluate the situation that has developed. This is an excellent way of giving yourself the chance to look at what sort of pitfall you've landed in. Another way of creating the space you need is simply to mention it, to openly describe what you're experiencing. Remember, as a Solution Focused coach, you strive to be transparent, so you are free to be honest about what you've noticed, as shown in this example:

> "I've noticed that we've somehow started talking about the problem again … while just a few minutes ago, we were working nicely together on those things you'd like to change. Did you notice that we both started feeling more energetic as we talked about your preferred change? Is it okay with you that we go back to that topic so that we can learn some more about what it is you want to do?"

When you use a question in this way, you guide the process in the direction you want. This is perfectly acceptable because you ask your client's permission. It would have been counterproductive to continue talking about problems. In a later chapter about the different aspects of coaching, you can read more about such ways of influencing the direction of the interaction.

A case study from practice: Bryan

Bryan, just turned 16, phones in to ask if he can come to my office later this afternoon. However, I'm fully booked, and Bryan has missed two earlier appointments without letting me know that he wouldn't be coming.

But I can hear the urgency in his voice, so I tell him he can come along at the end of the day, after my last appointment. He agrees and promises he'll be there on time.

It's 15:45 p.m., the last client but one has just left, and I'm waiting for my next client to arrive … and Bryan is already knocking at the door. He looks very nervous and is puffing furiously at a cigarette as he waits to be let in. An enormous cloud of tobacco smoke enters with him. I greet him and remind him about our phone conversation earlier this day. It's as if he doesn't hear me and pushes past me into my office and collapses into a chair.

Bryan takes off his coat and ignores what I say about not being available just yet. He shifts uneasily in his chair and leans forward with his elbows on his knees. He keeps shaking his head and is sniffing violently. It takes a moment before I realize that 'tough' young Bryan is struggling to keep his tears back. It's more than evident that he's going through something difficult that he seems unable to handle.

Coach: Okay, Bryan, I can see that something has happened that's hard for you to deal with ...

[Bryan nods]

Coach: It's good that you came. The time I can make available for you right now is very limited. But after my next appointment, we can talk further. So, if you'd please wait in the other room, then I'll have time for you shortly.

Bryan: Uh ... yes ... this just can't wait. I must talk to you now.

Coach: But Bryan, I have another appointment. The client should be arriving any moment now. I can't call her and tell her not to come – she's on her way right now as we speak.

Bryan: Oh yes? What's more important now: a stupid appointment or a matter of life and death? Because it's that serious right now!

Coach: *[Now slightly irritated]* Bryan, I fully understand that it's extremely important for you to speak with me straight away, but it's simply impossible. So what can I do for you in the next five minutes that I can make available that will help you in any way?

Bryan: *[now shouting in anger]* What sort of stupid deal is this? Always when I really need someone, then I can just forget about it. I'm leaving now. It doesn't make any difference any more. So what if they kill me? What do I care?

Bryan, an intelligent young man diagnosed with a borderline personality disorder, rants on for several minutes. I become aware that I cannot reach him at this point; I decide to try the tactic of reminding him of an earlier occasion when we were communicating much better with each other.

Coach: Bryan, when you called this morning, you asked very politely for an appointment. You seemed perfectly calm and in control. Even though I didn't really have any time for you today, I promised to make space for you at the end of the afternoon. Do you remember that you thanked me?

Bryan: Yes ... so what?

Coach: Well, *then* you were calm and polite. And that's one of the rea-
            sons I was willing to make the appointment with you. I have
            a suggestion: shall we keep the appointment we agreed on this
            morning? You can wait in the waiting room next door. There
            are things to read, and there's a computer I can turn on for you
            so that you can keep yourself occupied while waiting. And as
            soon as I'm ready, then I'll have plenty of time for you. Agreed?

Bryan, now somewhat calmed down, goes into the waiting room
and sullenly opens the door for the woman who has just knocked. She
thanks him in a friendly tone for opening the door. Bryan nods and
morosely takes his place in the waiting room.

In the next hour, I give my full attention to my female client while Bryan
waits. After escorting her to the door after her session, I turn to Bryan:

Coach: Right, Bryan, now it's time for us. Come along in and take a
            seat. I'll make us a cup of coffee, and we can take all the time
            we need. I appreciate that you gave me the space to deal with
            that last appointment. That helps me to stay calm and makes
            it possible for me to give you all the attention you need now.
            So, Bryan, what's cooking? How can I help you?

Clarification

Understandably, I was less than open toward Bryan when he called. It was
quite a challenge, considering my planning on an already-full day. I had,
moreover, not forgotten the two skipped appointments when I'd waited
fruitlessly for him to turn up. I was also aware of Bryan's tendency to exag-
gerate and blow up situations into a huge drama, which all too often only
existed between his ears.

It was challenging for me to stay open toward Bryan with such a track
record. In turn, Bryan is very sensitive. He is intelligent enough to sense
all this immediately and then to react from his chaotic state of panic. In
such a space, an accidental conflict is easily created. Luckily, I'm aware of
the dynamics of our interaction. Avoiding going into Bryan's accusations, I
steered the conversation back to an early moment that day when the communication between us was fine. When I reminded Bryan of this earlier smooth
exchange and complimenting him on it as well, the tone of the conversation
shifted. Bryan's resistance dissolved somewhat, and he became more open.

Overview

Falling suddenly into one of the pitfalls as described above can happen to
anyone at any moment. And yes, it can just as easily happen to experienced
coaches. They're human. Their advantage is, however, that they are usually

quick to recognize what is happening and know how to get back on track equally quick. It's a matter of asking the right questions, placing a compliment, timing … and indeed, a matter of observing and restoring rapport. It really helps to be aware of and let go of any personal judgment and to set aside personal beliefs.

Of course, I was annoyed, because I do think that Bryan, just like any other client, must keep to his appointments. But what I've learned to do is to be aware of my beliefs and associated feelings and be willing to set them aside as being of no use or value in the interaction with Bryan. That done, it became easier for me to reestablish contact with Bryan. And that's just a skill you, too, can develop.

All this implies that it's sometimes necessary to set aside any goals from your perspective, however important they may seem for the process at that moment. Using a Solution Focused approach to return to and restore the connection is a strategy that ultimately will be more effective. It prevents unnecessary wastage of valuable time *and* restores the relationship. It is perhaps the quality of the relationship that is so productive when working with young clients within Mission Possible. After all, without mutual trust, cooperation is simply impossible.

Working with Mission Possible in groups

A whole book could easily be devoted just to this aspect of working with the Mission Possible-program in group settings. After all, the dynamics of group processes are an inherent facet of working in a group. However, this book restricts its focus to a description of the various options when applying the program to working with a group of young people. For this moment, it is unimportant whether it's a group of young people who have volunteered to participate or whether it's a group in the formal setting of an institution.

Undesirable application

Although there are significant differences between these two groups when working with the Mission Possible-program, application is based on the same basic principles. Whatever the group, there's a strong preference for voluntary participation. If this point is ignored, there's a risk that the program is used as a tool for conditioning the participants; a constant struggle then develops to maintain a balance between correction and reward. Earning rewards by conforming to external expectations can quickly result in a situation in which the group participants manipulate the program's objectives.

Learning from real-life case histories

There is a great example of a group of adolescents in a closed youth-care institution. They managed to drive their group leaders crazy by constantly

Tools for the toolbox

Everything is useful. Every expression of emotion that you can observe in your client can in principle be experienced as a burden or even as a form of resistance. However, you can change your perspective and choose to see a quality instead:

- Angry – "I am involved and feel passionate about it."
- Sad – "I am able to express my feelings."
- Insolent – "I can stand up for myself."
- Silent – "I take time to think about where I stand."
- Overactive – "I'm very energetic."
- Rejecting – "I'm perfectly capable of determining what's right for me."
- Socially desirable – "I know exactly what is expected of me."
- Exaggerating – "I can act and have a sense of drama."
- Chaotic – "I experience many things all at once."
- Fearful – "I plan ahead, oversee possible consequences, and am alert."
- Lazy – "I use my energy sparingly."
- Shy – "I am observing from a distance."
- Lying – "I have a rich fantasy."
- Distrustful – "I am cautious."
- Dominant – "I'm a good leader."
- Demanding attention – "I want to be seen and heard."
- Obstinate – "I'm independent."
- Brash – "I am daring and courageous."
- Obsessive – "I am fascinated and have an eye for detail."
- Blabbermouth – "I am spontaneous."
- Hostile – "I only trust those who are worth it."
- Manipulative – "I very much want to reach my goal and know how."
- Fearful of failure – "I really want to do it well."
- Intimidating – "I want to do it my way."
- Depressed – "I overthink things in depth and I'm sensitive."

haggling over privileges and prescribed behavior. Helping clear up after a meal in exchange for extra computer time was bargained for per cup and saucer. And it should be clear that such a situation is *not* intended with the Mission Possible-program. As in this true case history, such action is totally useless as far as the personal development of the participants is concerned – a healthy customer relationship is missing, in which the clients 'own' both their problems *and* their solutions.

Prerequisites

Imagine a situation in which the group leadership starts looking at the possibility of implementing the Mission Possible-program. Their initial task is to ensure that the basic attitude of all personnel is oriented toward working in a Solution Focused manner. If not, then old problem-based systems of punishment and reward will continue to co-exist and undermine the Solution Focused approach of the Mission Possible-program. In that case, there's little chance of lasting success. Striving to take responsibility, as well as 'owning' the problem *and* the preferred change, is more than just an ideal picture: it is a prerequisite for genuine development and enduring success. Such long-term change requires a mindset that is focused on growth.

It goes virtually without saying that such an approach to change and growth can only be achieved in an institutional setting when both leadership and group participants are willing and able to make a shift in their mindset. A period of adjustment is unavoidable. These things take time and practice.

History and adaptation

Mission Possible was originally developed in Finland as a Solution Focused approach for such a residential setting. Ben Furman's original 16-step program has certainly proven to be useful. However, the program for educational guidance and nonresidential care of teenagers and adolescents has been thoroughly adapted in this book and the accompanying workbook.

The addition of Step 0 – establishing a customer relationship – to the program to ensure optimum motivation toward cooperation and independence is a feature that appears to be equally applicable in residential care. There's little chance a mindset focused on growth is going to develop under coercion.

The coach

When you work as a coach in a group, you should in no way underestimate your importance when it comes to affecting the mindset. You can positively influence the mood of the group by emphasizing learning goals instead of achievements. You can make it clear that making mistakes and experiencing setbacks are just normal parts of every learning process. It's up to you to set an example by showing that you, too, must do your best to learn new things and to achieve goals. You can show how things get more enjoyable as skills improve. You can encourage your group to do their best and to persevere.

And you can make it clear that everyone, without exception, can get better at something. By using your language as a conscious tool, you can show the group that there is something they cannot *yet* do but that it's a definite possibility if they cooperate in making it happen. It's up to you to look together with them at those things that have worked in the past and that could again work in the future. How things became successful in the past provides valuable information about how to proceed toward the future. Above all, it's the positive mindset focused on growth that fuels the motivation to take action.

Working on a common goal

One of the ways of working with Mission Possible in a group is to have the participants work together on reaching a common goal. This can be a goal that the group members propose themselves, but it can just as well be a goal described by a mentor or teacher who would like to encourage a specific change within the group. When the goal for the group has been suggested by someone from outside, then you'll first need to invest in establishing the group's collective motivation: the 'customer relationship'. If you recall the five psychological factors for autonomous motivation from the chapter on step 2, be fully aware that they apply equally well to a group as to an individual.

Determining a common goal

A complication when working with a group involves reaching consensus on what the common goal looks like. One way is to decide democratically, where the majority decides. However, negotiating and discussing can be perfectly effective in such groups. Applying tools such as described in Step 2: the advantages, can provide an excellent solution. Similarly, various creative work forms such as roleplay, visualizations in word and image, or discussions about social themes all can help the group to get clearer about viable common goals.

The important thing to realize is that you can use virtually everything that strengthens their motivation and gets them passionately involved and willing to cooperate. Even just brainstorming together about possible ways of working and how they can register and monitor their process can be highly stimulating. Depending on the size of the group, you might first choose to have them work in smaller subgroups.

A case study from the educational field: art class

In the art class, the teacher has given the students the assignment of making a drawing of themselves, a self-portrait. Some students get going right away, but other students dawdle and don't show much interest.

Student 1: How am I supposed to draw someone? I can't draw well. Can anyone draw a body for me? Otherwise it'll be useless.
Student 2: Just look in the mirror, stupid.

Student 1:   Mind your own business!

Student 2:   Then you shouldn't have asked, idiot!

Teacher: Come on, guys, what's the problem?

Student 1:   I'm willing to draw myself, but I don't know how. Could you perhaps give me a template that I can trace around?

Student 2:   Ha, ha, ha – that's a good one! Anyone can use a template. But then, what's the purpose? It wouldn't make much sense, this assignment. At least, that way I don't see it.

Teacher: Okay, okay, let's start out by taking a moment to talk about this together. What do you all think is the purpose of this assignment to draw yourself?

Student 1:   So that we learn to draw people?

Student 3:   You get to think about what you actually look like?

Student 2:   Yes – or how you *think* you look!

Student 4:   What's that got to do with it?

Teacher: Y'know, that's an interesting question. How *do* you think you look? And do you think that you look the same way that other people think you look?

Student 2:   Wow, that's deep! Yes, actually quite interesting, too. I think that I see myself differently from how others see me.

Teacher: Could it be useful to think about that for a while and then make a drawing to illustrate your conclusions?

Student 2:   Yes, I think so. It's all about the image you have of yourself.

Teacher: Is it important for you to think about this idea?

Student 3:   You bet! We already do that anyway. In some sense, we're all pretty busy thinking about this. I mean, isn't that basically the reason why we choose certain styles of clothing or a particular brand name or label?

A lively discussion gets going in the group about choices that the students make in how they determine their looks. There's a lot of laughing and joking. The term 'self-image' is often used. While the students are talking, the teacher silently lays out a wide variety of materials on the tables: paper, marker pens, paints, glue, magazines, pieces of cloth, and color samples as well as a video camera and a digital photo camera. She also places her laptop in the middle of one of the tables and connects it to the Internet.

The discussion quiets down and the students start asking questions about all the things the teacher has made available. The teacher, who has noticed some genuine curiosity among the students, explains that the students can use their own choice of materials to help them make a composition about themselves.

A student asks: Can we do this as a group assignment, Teacher?

The teacher answers: I don't see why not. Great idea!

Just a few minutes later, the group has decided to make a proper project of this initially simple drawing assignment, and they intend to make a video clip to post on YouTube.

The cooperation that now arises is quite remarkable. Plans are made and tasks assigned, and all students indicate what each of them would prefer to do. Some students appear to be born leaders, while others seem perfectly comfortable asking fellow students for help in carrying out their part of the project.

Independent motivation

The students regularly ask the teacher's advice when something arises that they themselves cannot resolve instantly. However, as soon as her counseling has brought matters back on course, the students continue to work independently again. Then the bell rings. It's time for a break.

Students: What? Is it time to stop already?

"Shit!" some student shouts.

Everyone helps with clearing up, and the classroom empties peacefully ... but not before the teacher has been pressured to reassure them that they can continue working on the project in the next lesson. "Maybe we can also work on this in our other lessons," one of the students calls out as he leaves.

Working with groups on individual goals

It is, of course, perfectly possible to work with a group, where each individual has his own goal. In this situation, you work with each client in the same way as if you were coaching just one client. It does place a certain burden on you to ensure that each separate program gets enough of your attention and support. For an experienced Mission Possible coach, this challenge should not be all that arduous, especially as young people are already able to do so much on their own.

Shared process

You can choose to do part of the program as a group process: Step 0, for example, is an excellent part of the program that is perfectly suited to a group discussion. The step concerning support is also very effective and agreeable as a group process. All group members can be each other's supporters during their individual program. This form of group support is in fact ideal for every Mission Possible client. Because all members of the group understand (from their own experience) what it means to work with the Mission Possible-program, little further explanation is required, *and* they are more understanding and supportive of each other. You might consider encouraging your individual clients to also attend group meetings to share about their mutual processes.

Independence and cooperation

Working on individual goals within a group in no way excludes cooperation. Quite the opposite: working on personal goals in a group context can provide young clients with a high degree of valuable support. An important advantage worth mentioning is that stigmatization simply doesn't take place. When each member of the group is working toward his own goal, he's no exception. The feeling that 'there is something wrong with me because I'm working toward a goal' simply cannot arise when everyone in the group has a goal he's aiming at. It would then be correct to say that working with the program should be perceived as simply another form of learning and development.

The role of the coach

It cannot be emphasized strongly enough that the framework provided by the Mission Possible-program is just a guideline. So much of what happens during the program depends on what your young client contributes and how he and you as his coach cooperate.

Questions, questions, and more questions

The most significant tool at your disposal as Mission Possible coach is simply asking questions. To help you, the accompanying Mission Possible workbook provides a fair summary of the most relevant questions. Please be clear about the fact that this is not complete and that it does not provide the only possible questions you can ask! There are so many more, but they *are* a useful guideline to help you maintain the best possible structure for the meetings with your client.

On course

The right questions are a great way of keeping on track with your client. Nevertheless, it is your client who basically determines the course's direction. Your task is important but limited. The less you are needed, the better. So if you find yourself on the edge of the chair, eager to work with your client, remember to relax, keep breathing, and just sit back. The client can take care of himself more than you think.

A relevant personal note

When I was younger, Bruce Lee was one of my biggest heroes. Although I was less interested in the fighting scenes than my older brother, I found myself fascinated by his silent presence in between. One of his quotations has always stayed with me. Although his quote was about teachers, it seems equally true for coaches.

"A great coach doesn't have fixed routines. Each moment requires from him a sensitive mind, constantly adapting.
"He must never impose his client to fit his favorite patterns.
"He protects his clients from his own influence. He never gives truth; he's a guide. He's a pointer to the truth that each client must find for himself.
"He doesn't teach anything. He just helps his client to explore himself."

This thoughtful statement, which I adapted in my memory of it, is a clear reminder about being as invisible as possible, like a Shaolin kung fu master who leaves no footprints behind in the snow. In practice, however, it's difficult. As a well-meaning coach, eager to help, it's all too easy to fall into the trap of behaving like a rescuer. If you try too hard to help, the client starts to feel inadequate and incompetent. And you will unintentionally rob him of his independence.

The trap of rescuing!

When coaching young clients, frequent silences and answers like "I've no idea" or "I don't know" are perfectly normal. Then it can well happen that your sense of unease will move you to try to help. This reflex action is hard to ignore! For this reason, it's important to be aware of the different roles that are available to you as a Solution Focused coach.

Different roles

Your primary role as the coach is being a helping guide, an equal helper to the client as a co-expert. But this equal role alone will in itself prove to be insufficient. Something else is often needed too, but what? Your basic attitude is clear: you're not there as an expert but as an equal partner with the task of *following* rather than *leading*. This is all true, but it is still worthwhile looking very closely at all the different coaching competences that you may need to be really effective in the interaction with your client.

Competences

There are four different areas of coaching competence that need to be looked at: coaching, guiding, training, and instructing. Only the first competence – coaching – fits completely within the framework of a Solution Focused process and is therefore the *preferable role*. But in all the situations in which this coaching role proves inadequate, something else is required. The basic attitude of Mission Possible already implies that the coach uses whatever works and fits the Solution Focused approach. However, there's a small problem: as soon as the coach starts doing anything else besides coaching, equality in the client–coach relationship – one of the main principles of Solution Focused coaching – ceases. Guiding, training, and instructing all imply that the client is in an inferior position, and those activities are then essentially *not* 'Solution Focused', because they don't meet the Solution Focused criteria.

Guiding

As a coach, you use your expertise to guide your client with what he needs in order to reach his goal. You clarify what is expected, or you invite him to make choices. You repeat, clarify, acknowledge, and persevere as ways to support his understanding of the process. Guiding also involves ensuring that the steps of the program are followed and session time is monitored – you maintain an overview of the processes involved.

Training

This is your opportunity to help your client acquire new skills, which you then ask him to practice with. You give him space to reflect on the positive feedback you share and offer him possibilities for self-improvement.

Instructing

Since your client may not yet have all the knowledge or necessary information he most likely needs, this is where you can offer it to him. You provide the necessary explanations and check with him what he already knows and is capable of so that he can integrate and use everything in the rest of his program. Teenagers and adolescents mostly gather their knowledge through consulting peers or the Internet, and you may find yourself often confronted with lack of information on important topics. In such cases, you can be of value by filling in the blanks.

Useful

Although these last three roles are fundamentally not Solution Focused, they are nevertheless highly relevant and appropriate. As a Mission Possible coach, therefore, you need to do more than *just* coach. Because these roles restrict the client's independence, it's important to start out by asking for your client's permission to use these roles. That's the first step. The second step is to explain, using positively formulated language, why this would be helpful. And as a final step, you must ensure that you keep the intrusion on your client's autonomy to a minimum so that he can be back in control as soon as possible.

Tools for the toolbox

1 Helping/coaching your client:

- Help your client to progress toward his preferred future.
- Help the client formulate what he wants to achieve.
- Help to visualize and to make available what is already working well.
- Help your client identify previous successes.
- Help your client choose possible next steps.
- Help the client acknowledge and monitor his progress.
- Align with the client's words and perception.

2 Guiding your client:

- This can be useful when management is necessary (e.g., time management, process monitoring)
- clarify your intentions and expectations in positive terms
- invite the client to determine how the desired result is achieved
- if necessary, patiently repeat and clarify expectations
- acknowledge and take the perspectives and reactions of your client seriously
- match friendliness to clarity
- match understanding to tenacity

3 Training/practicing with your client:

- Transfer new knowledge and skills to your client.
- Let the client decide for himself whether and how he'll use it
- Focus on usefulness, asking questions about usability.
- Utilize your client's existing skills and knowledge.
- Treat 'resistance' as an attempt to collaborate.
- Provide process-oriented positive feedback.
- Provide constructive opportunities for improvement.
- Let your client reflect himself.

4 Instructing your client:

- is helpful when a client doesn't yet know your intentions and lacks necessary information or experience.
- Explain your intention and reasons in positive words.
- Explore the client's resources, and make use of them.
- Allow the client autonomy as much as possible.
- Respect the client's choices as much as possible.
- Communicate to your client in a simple, patient, and encouraging way.

The limits of coaching

There will always be situations in which some form of (intensive) guidance will be necessary. Equally well, Solution Focused work with Mission Possible does not always provide answers to all the problems young people face. There are even situations where precisely this approach should be avoided (is contraindicated); then, a Solution Focused approach isn't the most suitable way to work. Think for a minute of situations where it is highly inadvisable to work this way, or at least initially is. The following four areas require a different approach, even if only at the beginning:

1 Extreme urgency or danger
2 Physical problems
3 Technical problems
4 Other standard procedures that have already proven to be effective

Of course, when a client is in deep despair and wants to harm himself or is even suicidal, then it is of little use or even dangerous to start talking about his preferred situations. The only appropriate answer from the client's perspective is for the pain he is in to stop. Also, when dealing with illness or physical ailments, a Solution Focused approach might seem attractive, but wouldn't you want your doctor to make an accurate diagnosis first? And, thinking of myself as a nontechnical person, it really is helpful, when the printer is refusing to do its work, to first check if it's plugged into the socket. And, obviously, when all goes well, why would you want to change anything?

Know your limits: consequences

As a coach, you should recognize your own limits as well as those of a coaching style while working with clients. When in doubt, referral is the best approach! If other professional assistance is recommended, then it's your task to see that it happens. You need to refer your client to a medical doctor, to the mental health authorities, a clinic, private practice, or another appropriate source of professional support that goes beyond what you have to offer.

Professional assistance

Referral is often viewed as very threatening by both the client and his parents. Then it is likely that your job as Solution Focused coach will be to facilitate the path to professional assistance. By paying attention to their concerns and the way in which these affect how they think and feel about the situation, you can play a useful if ancillary role in helping the referral to take place as smoothly as possible. In many cases, you can deploy Solution Focused coaching to work on and ease the grief and shame about the problem and the fear of the consequences of further professional assistance. The initial feelings can be minimized by continually focusing on the most preferred outcome, on what is already going well, and the willingness to cooperate based on expected improvement. A referral is certainly a radical intervention, so your sympathy and understanding will be beneficial as well.

Presence, here and now

Solution Focused work takes place, above all, in the present tense – more so than any other form of coaching or therapy. As a coach, you work with whatever it is that presents itself in the moment and, as described earlier, you pay little attention to what has happened in the past. If you do look back at previous events, it is primarily at an early stage, when you are discussing the problem and formulating the client's need for help. There's a good reason for doing this, namely to respect the emotions involved in the problem. Everyone needs to tell his story and feel he has been heard and understood. In principle, it is possible to work on a problem in a Solution Focused way without ever actually discussing the problem. However, the general effect is that the *problem* continues to draw attention and may continue to do so.

Listening from 'presence'

Feelings around the problem need to be expressed. That does not mean that you, as the coach, get involved in those feelings. It usually suffices just to give them some space and to acknowledge that they exist and are valid. Moreover, it helps if you 'hold the space,' an expression that describes how you remain present, listening attentively and sincerely, in the moment, fully focused on your client's sharing. It happens all too often that, while listening to your client, you'll start thinking about the next step or some association with what is being shared. Although it's totally understandable, your client will almost certainly sense your divided attention. Consciously or subconsciously, he will notice and interpret your (temporary) 'absence' in the moment. How he interprets your 'absence' depends on factors such as his worldview and self-image. But one thing is certain: for someone who seeks help in solving his problems, such a subconscious message is all too often registered as unwanted and negative and serves therefore to confirm previous, less agreeable experiences.

Trust relationship

Truly being present, with undivided attention in the moment, cannot be interpreted in any other way: the listener *is* present. The only message you send is "I am here for you now." And it is precisely this message that is the basis of a genuine trust relationship. In turn, that is the basis for open communication, in which asking questions – instead of giving answers – is the most important feature.

"You can't teach people anything. You can only help them to find their own way."

Galileo Galilei (1564–1642)

Dealing with emotions

Just because you create space for the feelings and emotions that arise from a problem does *not* mean that you give space to how these can complicate an interaction. There's always a certain risk involved in giving space. It is, for instance, just a short distance from the pure emotion and pain of experiencing a problem to complaining about it – or worse, to complaining about other people who are the cause of the problem. Conclusion: it's all right to create just 'enough' space.

How much space?

That raises the question: how much space *is* 'enough'? And how do you know when the point has arrived that enough attention has been paid to the problem and everything around it? It's not so easy to give an explicit answer to these questions. Each conversation, each coaching session, and each client is different and requires a different, appropriate approach. However, there are several clear indicators that help you to know when you have given 'enough' space and it's time to change direction in the conversation to a more Solution Focused approach.

Recognizing the moment

Perhaps the most obvious indicator is that of repetition of your client's story. You could then conclude that there's evidently nothing new to say. But be aware that it can also indicate that you have not done enough to make your client feel heard.

A second indicator is when your client begins to talk at length about matters that have little or no bearing on the problem. What he shares is not very relevant or is simply uninteresting for this coaching session.

These two indicators – the most common – let you know that there's been enough time and space for all aspects of the situation.

A third and very useful indicator is when you notice that your client starts complaining about the problem instead of talking about his feelings. And what precisely does this indicate to a Solution Focused coach? That it's time for something to change! This is then the perfect place to start looking closely at the preferred situation, at *what* precisely the client wants to be different in the future.

To miss such an indicator – a 'key' – may also be seen as a pitfall.

The power of being present

You can easily avoid this pitfall by giving your full attention to your client. You then optimize your ability to respond with alacrity and to guide the exchange in a more positive, fruitful direction. If you use the complaint as a signal of the desire for change, it becomes a key to the hitherto closed door to the future. Let's take a look at this with some examples.

The most effective way to prevent escalation – the problem beginning to seem even bigger, heavier – is simply not to respond to the complaints. Not to respond is, in this case, a sign of strength, not weakness. Your lack of response prevents the problem from becoming increasingly bigger and more painful. By using the complaints as signposts that your client really wants to change something, they become a key to the – until now – locked door to the preferred future. Below, you can read a number of real-life examples.

A case study from the educational field

Student (18): I'm totally pissed off that I only got an *F* for statistics. It's driving me crazy. Just because of that F, I've got too few credits and will probably have to repeat the whole semester. I know that, what with one thing and another, I hadn't prepared that well for this exam. But it's mainly because that twirt of a teacher just doesn't like me. What a (bleep) he is, to give me just an F, while I usually get much higher marks. If I get the chance, you can be sure I'll have my revenge on him.

The behavior of the student in this excerpt from a session is definitely an example of complaining. The feelings that are expressed don't all relate to the basic problem; they blame the teacher and shift responsibility away from the student. This student seems stuck in a mindset of complaining and blaming and seems not yet focused on any willingness to work toward change, none of which is useful in a Solution Focused approach.

Read now the same example, but with an alert and perfectly timed, Solution Focused intervention by the coach:

Alternative case study

Student (18): I'm totally pissed off that I only got an *F* for statistics. It's driving me crazy. Just because of that F, I've got too few credits and will probably have to repeat the whole semester.

Coach:	Indeed, I can fully understand that you're annoyed. That's a tough setback to deal with, and I can imagine that you'd prefer that it were different. But y'know, in the past, I've seen that you really *are* able to deliver better work. Have you any idea what you could possibly do in this situation?
Student:	Well, of course, I could simply accept what has happened and repeat the semester. Another possibility ... yes, maybe I could get to discuss the matter with my mentor and the statistics teacher. Who knows, maybe something could be arranged if I tell them about my circumstances. It would be great if I could get a second chance, and you could bet your life, I'd really work hard for it.
Coach:	Good, that sounds like you might have two excellent possibilities. Clever of you to immediately see there's even *more* than one option. What would the advantages of both options be for you?
Student:	Well, I'd rather not even think about the first ...
Coach:	Yes, I can understand that from your perspective! But because you don't know what the possibilities are, could it be a good idea to look more closely at both options? Maybe you'll even find some advantages to the first option.
Student:	Yes, I guess you're right ... Just to explore them.

The second version of the interview offers more opportunities for cooperation. With a well-placed question the coach intervenes in the ongoing complaining of the student, which can no longer be seen as useful. It is just more of the same and isn't leading to any solutions. Creating a shift in mindset steers the student toward growth and offers to change the outcome of a feared future into new opportunities for improvement.

Emotions

It is very useful when you as a coach are alert to channel the emotions that your client expresses. Since adolescents are still developing emotionally, they tend to experience intense emotional states, such as outrage, anger, and resentment. They confirm and validate their sense of who they are by acting and reacting to their experiences, not always being aware of the extent to which their emotions filter their perception of reality. These emotional outbursts calm down as you bring attention back to the here and now, where focus returns to relevant themes.

Waiting out the wave

The sheer nature of an emotion is one of being a wave, with a low and a high, taking time to completely unfold and reveal its' entire nature. Generally speaking, in an emotion, there is no 'truth' in the moment. Making decisions at any point in that wave will most certainly be regretted in retrospect. Only waiting out the entire wavelength can bring clarity and understanding in hindsight. These waves involve only either the past or the future. They concern matters that have already happened or that may or may not happen at some future moment. They are seldom relevant to the here and now, and, if so, tend to be very short-lived.

Comparison

To clarify the effect of emotions, imagine a little boat at sea during a hurricane. Towering waves threaten to engulf the boat and throw it back and forth while keeping the helmsman caught in a fierce battle against the pounding waves. The captain struggles to keep the boat afloat, let alone succeeding to steer it into the wind. *That* is the effect of being controlled by emotions, where logical thinking is of little practical use. The running emotional wave blocks access to the rational mind. Powerless in that chaos, the 'boat' is pushed around out of control among the huge waves. However, take the time to dive deeper under the storm-tossed surface, ignoring the cause of the emotion, and discover a space to calm down and look around more objectively. Under the storm-swept surface, the sea is surprisingly peaceful. It's precisely there that it's possible to get in touch again with the available resources, innate and acquired qualities, skills, and existing experiences of success that ease the path to the goal. Only when you stay as much as possible in the here and now are these resources optimally accessible and available for use.

Experiment

'Mindfulness' is a simple way of learning to be in the here and now that can be applied in many different situations. While you walk (cycle, drive) name all the things you come across. You can do this in your head, but it's more effective if you speak out loud. If at that moment you can't think of what something is called, just say "Thing!" instead of stopping and searching your mind for the right word. Practice this for at least five to ten minutes a day.

If you notice that your thoughts stray – "… chair, table, curtain, oh dear, they could do with washing …" – just go straight on just naming the things you see *without any further judgment.*

You can do this as a separate, daily exercise as well as integrate it into regular activities like clearing up the kitchen, changing the bedcovers, cycling to work, taking a ride in a bus, and so on.

See if you can notice what the effect is after doing this exercise for a few days or weeks in a row. You might even want to keep a diary describing what you observe and discover.

Helping or inviting?

Working as a Solution Focused coach requires you both to make a considerable shift in your mindset and to adopt a different basic attitude. Your coachee is as much as possible an equal partner with you, his helper. He owns his problems, his dreams for the future, his goals and the solutions. You as coach – or therapist – follow his process as if from one step behind him, looking over his shoulder. It sounds very simple, so read on for an example to clarify this idea.

Maybe the following comparison will provide more insight into this way of working. Imagine you have a child who has just learned how to ride a bike. For a couple of days now, he's been making short, wobbly rides on his new bike. You still help him get on the bike and give him a push to get him going. You follow him with a sense of pride yet with some concern that all will go well and see the wobbly movements of the handlebars as he cycles away from you. As he continues to practice and become increasingly confident, the day arrives when you decide it's all right for him to cycle next to you on his way to school.

As you cycle together, you continue to encourage and compliment him. All is going well. You adjust your speed to that of your proud child as he pedals away and you keep your front wheel behind his. For a fraction of a second, however, your attention wanders, you peddle a little faster, and your front wheel is all of a sudden ahead of your child's front wheel. Almost immediately, your child starts to cry in panic:

"Mum [Dad], not so fast! I can't keep up!"

As soon as you respond by slowing down, your child relaxes and feels confident again. When you stay just a little behind your child's bike, even if it's just a few centimeters, he feels supported and exudes self-confidence. When you get even slightly ahead, the sense of support disappears, and doubt in his ability starts arising.

The next real-life story illustrates this style of working.

A case study from practice: Josh and Marsha continuation

It's time again for Marsha and Josh to come for a session. You've met them before, earlier on in this book. Two weeks ago, they requested an appointment together. Apart from the first meeting some five months ago, when they came with their mother, they've always had separate sessions. It is their initiative, and I am quite curious.

In the meantime, Josh has taken some important steps on his way to a healthy change in his behavior. Through his school, where's he is educated for a technical profession, he's now getting some work experience at a large local bike shop.

Rediscovering passion and joy

On several occasions, he's spoken enthusiastically about what he's learning, as he feels totally at home there. Since he enjoys social contact so much, he feels very comfortable with the informal daily interaction with complainers and colleagues. He also takes enormous pleasure in repairing bikes and feels that he is genuinely appreciated, both by his boss and the complainers. His boss is very positive about him, and the reports from school indicate that he's making excellent progress.

Josh himself told me that the situation at home is much improved. The relationship with his mother, who works extremely hard to support the family on her own, is now much more relaxed and agreeable. When I asked him how that happened, he replied that they now talk more often about his dad. Josh's father, who passed away some time ago, has left an enormous gap in their family. For Josh, this painful loss was his reason to act out his grief on the rest of the family. For a long time, it was barely possible for him to talk about the loss of his father and his grief.

Coach: How are things for you now, Josh?

Josh: Actually pretty good, Coach. We talk surprisingly often about my dad now. Sometimes we even laugh about some of the stories from the times when my dad was still here. We laugh a bit, cry a bit, sometimes all at once, y'know … There's so much I'd actually forgotten, but it's nice to hear things, although they sometimes make me feel sad, too.

Coach: I can imagine, Josh. Do you think it helps you nonetheless, this sort of conversation?

Josh: Yes, it really does. It feels okay.

Marsha: Well, not always. Sometimes you're not in the mood, and you get angry and walk away.

Josh: True. And it makes sense, doesn't it? You're not always in the mood either, are you? But at least I don't get mad at you any more, do I?

Marsha: Yes, that you don't do anymore.

Coach: What has changed for you, Marsha?

Marsha: Well, it's more or less the same as for Josh. Sometimes we just talk about Dad now. The three of us together, and we just share stories about him, about how it used to be, when Dad was still with us. Sometimes we look at old holiday photos. Oh yes, and recently we even looked at some of Dad's things together with Mum.

Coach: How has that helped?

Restored relations

Marsha: Well, we're certainly much more honest with each other. At first, nobody really wanted the others to know what was bothering us. I avoided the subject because Josh was always getting so angry. Sometimes I was simply afraid of his anger. Especially since Mum had no idea how to deal with it. They'd both begin to scream at each other and so on. And then I'd be there, caught between, feeling all alone and sad. So I just kept quiet. And then, there're always these arguments with Josh, even if I said nothing. Just coming near him, he'd get onto me ... I felt like a punch bag, you know what I mean.

Josh: Oh, you're exaggerating. Surely it wasn't that bad?

Marsha: You'd better believe it!

Coach: Okay, so how are things between you now? What's different since the first time you came here?

[Silence. The brother and sister exchange sheepish glances]

Marsha: Well, quite a lot has changed. There are almost no more fights unless Josh steals my things. Then I *do* get angry. Even Mum says he should keep out of my room.

[Both laugh and kick each other in a friendly way]

Coach: And for you, Josh? What's different for you?

Josh: Oh, well, everything. I even feel like doing things again.

Coach: Wow, that's quite something! No arguments, or at least almost none anymore. Josh feels motivated again. I see you both laughing and teasing each other like friends. It looks like you're a team now. And your Mum, what does she see that's changed?

Together: The same!

Marsha: Mum just said last week what an enormous difference there is with six months ago. Very often it's fun simply being together.

A 'different' Marsha

It is quite amazing to see how often Marsha takes the initiative to contribute in this conversation. In the very first session, it was really Josh who was the active conversationalist, while Marsha was very timid. I compliment her on how she takes her space in this conversation.

Coach: Marsha, I'm delighted at how you present yourself in here today. You've certainly learned to express yourself more. Tell me how you learned to do that. In our email exchanges, you've mentioned it briefly, but it's really great for me to see that you now take the space you need. What has helped you to be able to do this?

Becoming aware of what worked?

Marsha: First and foremost, it's simply that Josh isn't such a nuisance any longer, so I dare to speak out more. And also, I really had set myself the goal for my Mission Possible-program to get better at standing up for myself. You advised me to make a list, remember? A list of all the things I could learn in order to be able to stand up for myself. And it really helped.

Coach: Tell me more ...

Marsha: Oh, there were so many things, too many to mention. I think there were at least 30 things on my list. Most of them I already mastered. So it turned out to be quite easy in the end.

Coach: Do you remember what it was that you started working on?

Marsha: Yes, I do – I had to let my voice be heard.

Josh: Yeah, that was a good laugh. She often practiced in front of the mirror. Screaming sometimes. Horrible to listen to ...

[Josh rolls his eyes, and we all laugh at his outburst]

Summarizing

Coach: So if I understand correctly, it's been a worthwhile process looking at precisely what you needed to do for yourself in order to be heard. And apparently everybody else had to put up with it, right?

Marsha: That's right, and it worked really fast. Nobody was used to me being like that.

Coach: And what was that like for you, Josh, that your sister changed so much?

Josh: Had to get used to it, of course. But I remember also, it was actually pretty cool. Before, she was crying all the time ... being a real mollusk. And that's why I got angry. I thought she was acting so retarded. When she stopped behaving like that, things were different.

Coach: It's wonderful to see how things can work out like this. I want you both to know it's been a real pleasure for me to see how you've changed and grown. I feel I've hardly had to do anything. Marsha, in your emails, you told me very conscientiously about what was going on. All those emails have become a terrific sort of diary covering your entire journey.

And Josh, you popped in here regularly. As you yourself said, you're not much of a writer. And you kept me nicely up to date on all that happened. Of course, that certainly counts as a pretty good logbook. I've also had good contacts with your school. I have the feeling that you've both achieved a great deal in a relatively short period of time. After all, you've had to process a pile of difficult stuff to get where you are now. And you've both been very creative in dealing with it all. What else would you like to discuss with me in the remaining time? We've looked back on your journeys – was that useful for both of you?

Josh: Of course, I think we've been through the most important things ...

Marsha: Well, wait a minute – I feel we've not covered everything with me. In our e-mails, we did. But it certainly feels good, too, to have a session all together. That's the finishing touch for me!

Coach: Beautiful! And yes, you made this appointment together. And we still have some time left. Is there anything more you would like to discuss?

New ideas

[They look at each other, laughing, with a "will you, or shall I?" glance]

Marsha: Okay, I will. I was talking anyway. Well, we want to do this with our friends. Can we?

Josh: C'mon, silly, you need to explain what you're talking about.

Marsha: Oh yes ... well, in the time we've been doing the program, we've actually talked a lot with our friends – especially that stuff about having supporters – but with other people, too. And they're all pretty curious. They ask all sorts of questions. We've shown them that new workbook – it wasn't available when we started on our program. We just had a printed copy from your computer. But now there are lots of questions about it. Can we also do this with a group, I mean with our friends? We think we'd like to.

Coach: Yes, that's certainly possible. You're correct in having understood that working in a group is one of the options. Do you have any ideas of your own as to how it could work?

Josh: I think we'd first have to think of a common goal.

Coach: Yes, that's one way of doing it. And it's also possible for everyone to have his or her own goal and still work together as a group. We could go over and sit at the big table and work out some creative ideas for a plan. What do you think?

Marsha: Can we do that with the whole of our group?

Coach: I can't see why not ...

Josh: And can we keep in touch using a group app or email in case we have any questions?

Coach: What do you think? Would that work for you?

Planning to celebrate

Marsha: Yes, I think so. We now know how the program works. Come to think of it, didn't we forget something?

Josh: No, I didn't. I was ready to say something about it.

Coach:	Ah, you're referring to the celebration? Of course, we still have to discuss that and make plans. I could never forget, but I'm glad you bring it up now.
Josh:	Just as we stated in the beginning, we want to keep it in the family, since our Mission Possible was all about our family. But we also had quite a few supporters from outside our family, like friends, aunts and uncles, schoolteachers, and our mentors. Even neighbors. Of course, we want them to share in the celebration, too.
Marsha:	And not to forget, you! We've written an invitation, and we plan to send it by e-mail. Mums said it's okay for us to do it at home at the end of the school semester. That's in three weeks.
Coach:	Great, that will give everyone plenty of time to come.
Josh:	Yes, that's what we think too. And we are going to keep it a surprise as to what you may expect. You'll see. It will be nice, I promise.
Coach:	So, I see that you have already prepared yourself well. It will be my pleasure to be part of it.

The coach does not know in advance what Josh and Marsha will present in the session. Their goals for the conversation become apparent along the way.

The coach's task is to conduct a conversation from an attitude of moving along, giving support, and being inquisitive. This concept, called 'coaching from one step behind the shoulder' (Steve de Shazer and Insoo Kim Berg), keeps the coach in a constant state of 'not-knowing.' There is nothing to hold onto that can support you to give structure to your coaching. There is little more to do but simply *be present*. In the here and now, everything that is necessary and useful for the process will present itself and become available. You do not apply any method. Nothing in the client's process is formed according to any theory or model. Nor do you anticipate any next step.

Experiment

How does it feel to 'coach from one step behind'? Here follows a two-part exercise to give you a taste of this approach. The first part lets you experience *leading* and *following*. The second part is designed to help you become more aware of the nonverbal and 'energetic' signals that indicate the direction your partner in this exercise wants to go. By remaining closely in contact, you can very subtly guide him … but the remarkable thing is that subtle guidance is actually a form of following!

The exercise is done in two parts with a partner. It's a good idea to have a timer available to keep track of the time. In silence, stand almost opposite each other so that you can both raise your right hand, palm outward. Either lightly grasp each other's hand or just place your palms against each other, whatever feels comfortable. Staying silent helps you to concentrate and make the exercise more effective. Agree who is to begin – who is to lead and who is to follow. You're going to repeat every part of the exercise so that you can both experience leading and following.

Part 1

Set the timer for two minutes and place your hands as described above. Partner 1, the leader, gently moves his hand in all directions he wants, and Partner 2 does his best to follow without losing the contact. Observe carefully how you feel as leader or as follower. When the timer goes off, relax and give your arm a little shake to release any tension. Now change over and repeat this part.

Part 2

Set the timer again for two minutes and place your palms together again. As before, Partner 1 moves his hand and Partner 2 follows, but now with this difference: Partner 1 (leader) does not determine where he will guide Partner 2. Instead, he tries to sense, through the palm of his hand, where the other *wants* to be led. Be aware, each partner in his own role, how it feels to lead or guide while at the same time 'listening' intently to where the other would like to go.

The exercise stops when the timer goes off. After shaking out the arm and relaxing, you switch roles and repeat this part of the exercise.

Questions for the discussion afterward

- What feels different in the second part of the exercise?
- What, if anything, has changed in the movements?
- Which role and which part of the exercise is more enjoyable to you, and why?

Observations

If all has gone well, both partners notice that the energy between them is different in the second part. The movements are smaller, and the attention for each other has changed and is perhaps more intense. There's a shift in awareness, and you can even experience a sort of trance or 'altered consciousness.'

During the first part, attention is focused on the other partner; this is especially true for the follower. However, in the second part, the attention of both partners is split between the other partner and the personal inner experience.

So both partners observe two processes at once: one is the process of the other, and the other is the personal inner process.

For experienced observers, there *is* a possible third process that you may notice. That process is that of the inner observer who, with a birds-eye view, maintains an objective overall view of the different processes at once. It is called a 'meta-level view.' This inner observer can give you much support in making the decisions in a coaching or therapy session.

The only sources of support you have in following and understanding this exercise are the basic attitude inherent to Solution Focused principles and the structure of the program. Remember, too, that the principles and program do not need to follow a strictly chronological pattern. After all, your client is the one who determines where the process ultimately leads to and precisely when he will take the necessary steps involved.

Your task as coach is to witness the process as it unravels, as far as possible without any judgments or projections. Your attention stays focused on what works for your client, *not* on what works for you! It would therefore be true to say that the Solution Focused approach involves inviting and facilitating rather than helping. It requires you to be constantly present if you wish to invite your client to discover, research, and apply his own abilities and resources. You create and facilitate a space in which the process develops and takes place in a time frame that suits your client and his needs. Perhaps one of the most frequently applied as well as desirable interventions of the Solution Focused coach is simply counting up to 20 in your mind, and then even some more. In a funny sense, Solution Focused work is ideally suited to 'lazy' coaches – do as little as possible! The smallest possible essential intervention and the smallest change have the most effect.

**"When the best coach's work is done, the client will say:
I did it myself."**

As you're gradually discovering in this book, Mission Possible is an approach that requires your utmost presence, an alert awareness, along with a critical listening faculty, eyes and ears that miss nothing, brains that are flexible and can make quick decisions and changes of direction, lots of patience, respect, and – to cap it all – the willingness to look inside, compassion, and forgiveness for all mistakes you make.

For all that the rewards are huge when you see how your clients take enormous strides in a relatively short period of time, take increasingly more responsibility for their lives, own their problems and the associated solutions, and, with newly acquired or rediscovered self-confidence, dare to look toward the future.

Epilogue

At the conclusion of this latest edition about the Mission Possible-program, I express the sincere hope that you will have developed or revitalized your optimistic view of working with adolescent clients. I also hope that you have perhaps (re)discovered how much there is to learn from how they view the world and their ways of doing things. When you coach them in gaining insight and acquire an overview of their lives, both their experiences as well as yours are enriched. If there is one thing that I have learned over the years from working with people of all ages, it is the simple fact that I myself have learned a great deal from them. Above all, it is teenagers and young adults who regularly confront me with my own pitfalls and behavioral patterns. They do not always adopt the same obedience as younger children tend to do but are mainly absorbed in discovering their own identity and path in life. And they regularly create a merciless and unflattering mirror for my own functioning and shortcomings. Just as the fluorescent lighting in the fitting room of many clothing stores is often horribly revealing, so too do these adolescents reveal – mostly unintentionally – precisely those areas in which my own performance still has room for improvement. What I willingly share with you is this: if you are willing to continue working on yourself with similar courage and youthful energy as your clients do, then you'll learn to be comfortable with each 'confrontation.' You'll discover that they are actually a precious gift. True, all too often, the gift is wrapped in unusual or awkward packaging, but a closer look usually reveals a valuable gem.

I also hope that you've become more familiar and comfortable with the Mission Possible-program as well as with Solution Focused work in general. Maybe you have even become convinced of how useful Mission Possible can be, especially when working with young clients who are faced with a need to set goals, change their behavior, develop new skills, or learn to improve them. You now know how to apply the steps to help them solve their problems. You have seen how you can support them while they deal with inevitable change and use it to their advantage. Although the focus of this book is on working with individual young people, you've also gained insight in how the same rules apply to groups.

And as you become increasingly familiar with using this program, you might start considering this: it is, of course, a compilation of fairly 'technical' rules for supporting change and for the practical guidance of personal growth. But it is more than just that; it is also a philosophy of change. The program provides a clear vision of how problems can be constructively resolved. It provides insight into the psychological factors of motivation and how these can be deployed to strengthen the client's motivation. It is a way of consciously activating participation of the client's environment, getting his friends and relatives to actively become involved in his adventure. That social network is an otherwise-untapped reservoir of possibilities that help to turn the client's preferred future into a reality.

It is my hope that you – as teacher, mentor, coach, or therapist – will have the opportunity to integrate the ideas of Mission Possible into your work with teenagers and young adults. Then you, too, will experience how energizing this approach is. True, I'll be happy even if you just feel attracted by the basic principles of Solution Focused work and that you find a way to apply them in your work or your personal life.

I would love to hear your experiences when working with Mission Possible so that I can continue to improve the application of this program. The Mission Possible-program continues to be a process of ongoing co-creation and cooperation.

A number of tools associated with the Mission Possible-program have since been developed in the Netherlands, such as an attractive illustrated poster (A3 and A1) with all the steps and an illustrated workbook for clients to help them to monitor their progress. All of these will soon become available in English too.

Supporting literature

Dutch

Bannink, F. (2007). *Gelukkig zijn en geluk hebben. Zelf oplossingsgericht werken*. Amsterdam: Harcourt.

Bannink, F. (2008). *Oplossingsgerichte vragen. Handboek oplossingsgerichte gespreksvoering*. Amsterdam: Harcourt.

Berg, I.K. & Dolan, Y. (2002). *De praktijk van oplossingen. Gevalsbeschrijvingen uit de oplossingsgerichte gesprekstherapie*. Lisse: Swets & Zeitlinger.

Berg, I.K. & Steiner, T. (2004). *Het spel van oplossingen. Oplossingsgerichte psychotherapie voor kinderen*. Amsterdam: Harcourt.

Berg, I.K. & Szabo, P. (2006). *Oplossingsgericht coachen*. Zaltbommel: Thema.

Blokland, T. (2001). *Stand van zaken. Waarom de populariteit van Putnam zorgwerkend is*. Research paper. Groningen: University of Groningen Press.

Cauffman, L. & van Dijk, D. (2009). *Handboek oplossingsgericht werken in het onderwijs*. Den Haag: Boom Onderwijs.

de Hart, J. (Red.) (2002). *Zekere banden. Sociale cohesie, leefbaarheid en veiligheid*. Den Haag: Sociaal en Cultureel Planbureau.

de Jong, P. & Berg, I.K. (2001). *De kracht van oplossingen. Handwijzer voor oplossingsgerichte gesprekstherapie*. Lisse: Swets & Zeitlinger.

Dolan, Y. (2000). *Stap voor stap. De zoektocht voorbij trauma en therapie op weg naar een leven van geluk*. Baarn: Hb Uitgevers.

Durrant, M. (2006). *Oplossingsgericht werken met jongeren en hun gezin. Een creatieve benadering van de residentiële hulpverlening*. Antwerpen/Apeldoorn: Garant.

Durrant, M. (2007). *Creatieve oplossingen bij gedragsproblemen op school*. Antwerpen/Apeldoorn: Garant.

Furman, B. (2006). *De methode Kids'Skills. Op speelse wijze vaardigheden ontwikkelen bij kinderen*. Soest: Uitgeverij Nelissen.

Furman, B. (2009). *Mijn Kids'Skills vaardighedenboek*. Huizen: Uitgeverij Pica.

Furman, B. & Ahola, T. (2009). *Reteaming*. Barneveld: Uitgeverij Nelissen.

Furman, B. & Beumer-Peeters, C. (2010). *Werkboek voor de jongere Mission Possible*. Huizen: Uitgeverij Pica.

Geurtz, J. (2004). *Het einde van de opvoeding*. Amsterdam: Ambo.

Heuves, W. (2006). *Pubers. Ontwikkeling en problemen*. Assen: Van Gorcum.

Isebaert, L. & Dumoulin, J.P. (1999). *Drink wijzer, een praktische gids voor verantwoord alcoholgebruik*. Leuven: Van Halewyck.

Jackson, P. & McKergow, M. (2002). *Oplossingsgericht denken*. Zaltbommel: Thema.

Kabat-Zinn, J. & Kabat-Zinn, M. (2001). *Met kinderen groeien. Over aandacht in opvoeding en gezin*. Rotterdam: Asoka.

Måhlberg, K. & Sjöblom, M. (2008). *Oplossingsgericht onderwijzen*. Antwerpen/ Apeldoorn: Garant.

Metcalf, L. (2007). *Oplossingsgerichte groepstherapie. Werken met groepen in privé-praktijk, scholen, bedrijven en behandelprogramma's*. Amsterdam: Harcourt.

Osho (2008). *Met open armen. Hier en nu bewust leven*. Amsterdam: Osho publikaties.

Roeden, J. & Bannink, F. (2007). *Handboek oplossingsgericht werken met licht verstandelijk beperkte cliënten*. Amsterdam: Harcourt.

Rosenberg, M.B. (2002). *Geweldloze communicatie. Ontwapenend en doeltreffend*. Rotterdam: Lemniscaat.

Tolle, E. (2001). *De kracht van het Nu*. Deventer: Ankh-Hermes.

Tolle, E. (2003). *De stilte spreekt*. Deventer: Ankh-Hermes.

van Dam, L. (2007). *Het reflecting team-intervisiemodel*. Soest: Uitgeverij Nelissen.

Visser, C. (2016). *Progressiegericht werken. Betekenisvolle vooruitgang*. Driebergen: Just-In-Time Books.

Wittebrood, K. & van Dijk, T. (2007). *Aandacht voor de wijk. Effecten van herstructurering op de leefbaarheid en veiligheid*. Den Haag: Sociaal en Cultureel Planbureau.

English

Almaas, A.H. (1996). *The Point of Existence: Transformations of Narcissism in Self-Realization*. Boston: Shambhala Publications.

Almaas, A.H. (2004). *The Inner Journey Home: Soul's Realization of the Unity of Reality*. Boston: Shambhala Publications.

Bandura, A. (1997). *Self-Efficacy: The Exercise of Control*. New York: W.H. Freeman.

Bavelas, A., Bavelas, J., & Schaefer, B.A. (1980). Using Echo Technique to Construct Student-Generated Faculty Evaluation Questionnaires. *Teaching of Psychology*, 7(2), 83–86.

Bee, H. & Boyd, D. (2002). *Lifespan Development*. Boston: Allyn & Bacon.

Berg, I.K. & Shilts, L. (2002). *WOWW (Working on What Works: Coaching Teachers to Do More of What's Working)*.

Berg, I.K. & Steiner, T. (2003). *Children's Solution Work*. New York: W.W. Norton & Co.

Bertolino, B. (2003). *Change-Oriented Therapy with Adolescents and Young Adults*. New York: W.W. Norton & Co.

Bowlby, J. (1988). *A Secure Base: Parent-Child Attachment and Healthy Human Development*. New York: Basic Books.

Brazelton, T.B. (1992). *Touchpoints*. New York: Addison-Wesley.

British Columbia Centre for Ability (1998). *Partnerships in Addressing Challenging Behavior*. Vancouver: S.1.

Brown, B. (1999). *Soul Without Shame: A Guide to Liberating Yourself from the Judge Within*. Boston: Shambhala Publications.

Childre, D. (1992). *Teen Self Discovery: Helping Teens Find Balance, Security & Esteem*. Boulder Creek, CA: Planetary Publications.

Deci, E.L. & Ryan, R.M. (1985). *Intrinsic Motivation and Self-Determination in Human Behavior*. New York: Plenum.

Deci, E.L. & Ryan, R.M. (2016). *Self-Determination Theory: Basic Psychological Needs in Motivation, Development, and Wellness*. New York: The Guilford Press.

De Jong, P. & Berg, I.K. (2002). *Interviewing for Solutions* (2nd edn). Pacific Grove, CA: Brooks/Cole.

De Shazer, S. (1991). *Putting Difference to Work*. New York: W.W. Norton.

De Shazer, S. & Dolan, Y. (2007). *More than Miracles: The State of the Art of Solution Focused Brief Therapy*. Binghamton, NY: Haworth Press.

Dunst, C.J. (2000). Revisiting "Rethinking Early Intervention". *Special Education*, 20, 95–104.

Dunst, C.J. & Trivette, C.M. (1998). Helping, Helplessness, and Harm. In J.C. Witt, S.N. Elliott, & F.M. Gresham (Eds), *Handbook of Behavior Therapy and Education*. New York: Plenum Press.

Dweck, C. (2007). *Mindset: The New Psychology of Success*. New York: Random House.

Freeman, J., Epston, D., & Lobovits, D. (1997). *Playful Approaches to Serious Problems: Narrative Therapy with Children and Their Families*. New York: W.W. Norton.

Furman, B. (2002). *Kids'Skills Parent Manual*. Helsinki: Helsinki Brief Therapy Institute.

Furman, B. (2002). *Kids'Skills: The Solution-Oriented Approach to Solving Children's Problems*. Helsinki: Helsinki Brief Therapy Institute.

Furman, B. & Ahola, T. (1992). *Solution Talk: Hosting Therapeutic Conversations*. London: BT Press.

Furman, B. & Ahola, T. (2002). *The Twin Star Book: A Solution Focused Approach to Improving the Psychosocial Environment of the Work Place*. Helsinki: Helsinki Brief Therapy Institute.

Furman, B. & Ahola, T. (2007). *Change Through Cooperation*. Helsinki: Helsinki Brief Therapy Institute.

Furman, B. & Ahola, T. (2010). *Creating Solution Focused Working Environments*. Helsinki: Helsinki Brief Therapy Institute.

Glasser, W. (1968). *Schools Without Failure*. New York: Harper Collins.

Glasser, W. (1998). *Choice Theory: A New Psychology of Personal Freedom*. New York: HarperCollins.

Lethem, J. (2002). Brief Solution Focused Therapy. *Child and Adolescent Mental Health*, 7(4), 189–192.

Levinthal, C.F. (2005). *Drugs, Behavior, and Modern Society*. Boston: Pearson.

Long, B. (1998). *Raising Children in Love, Justice and Truth*. London: Barry Long Books.

Måhlberg, K. & Sjöblom, M. (2002). *Solution Focused Education: For a Happier School*. Stockholm: Mareld.

Matthews, N. (2010). *The Friend: Finding Compassion With Yourself*. Washington, DC: O Books.

McKergow, M. & Clarke, J. (2005). *Positive Approaches to Change: Applications of Solutions Focus and Appreciative Inquiry at Work*. Cheltenham: Solutions Books.

Melton, G.B. (1995). *The Individual, the Family, and Social Good: Personal Fulfillment in Times of Change*. Lincoln, NB: University of Nebraska Press.

Miller, S.D., Duncan, B.L., & Hubble, M.A. (1997). *Escape from Babel: Towards a Unifying Language for Psychotherapy*. New York: W.W. Norton.

Neufeld, G. & Maté, G. (2004). *Hold On to Your Kids: Why Parents Matter*. Toronto: Alfred A. Knopf.

Nichols, M.P. & Schwartz, R.C. (2004). *Family Therapy: Concepts and Methods*. Boston: Pearson Education, Inc.

Putnam, R. (2000). *Bowling Alone: The Collapse and Revival of American Community*. New York: Simon & Schuster.

Rubin, H.R. & Rubin, I.S. (2005). *Qualitative Interviewing: The Art of Hearing Data*. Thousand Oaks, CA: Sage.

Safran, S.P. & Oswald, K. (2003). Positive Behavior Supports. Can Schools Reshape Disciplinary Practice? *Exceptional Children, 69*(3), 361–373.

Selekman, M.D. (1997). *Solution Focused Therapy with Children*. New York: Guilford Press.

Settersen, R.A. (2002). *Invitation to the Life Course: Towards New Understandings of Later Life*. New York: Baywood.

Sheldon, K.M. & Krieger, L.S. (2014). Walking the Talk. Value Importance, Value Enactment, and Well-Being. *Motivation and Emotion, 5*(38), 609–619.

Shonkoff, J.P. & Phillips, D.A. (Eds) (2000). *From Neurons to Neighbourhoods: The Science of Early Childhood Development*. Washington, DC: National Academy Press.

Wubbolding, R. (2002). *Reality Therapy for the 21st Century*. Philadelphia: Brunner-Routledge.

Interesting Solution Focused websites

www.benfurman.com
www.brandnewway.nl: author's website
www.brief.org.uk
www.erickson-foundation.org
www.kidsskillsonline.com
www.mri.org
www.reteaming.com
www.thesolutionfocus.com

Available for free: Kids'Skills app

Available in English, Chinese, Dutch, Finnish, Swedish, Danish, German, Spanish and Russian; available for Apple, Google Play, and APKPure (for Android)

Index

Note: page numbers in *italic* indicate a figure, and page numbers in **bold** indicate a table on the corresponding page.

For Product Safety Concerns and Information please contact our EU
representative GPSR@taylorandfrancis.com
Taylor & Francis Verlag GmbH, Kaufingerstraße 24, 80331 München, Germany

9 780367 747237